MARK BRANDON READ

CHOPPER 2

HOW TO SHOOT FRIENDS AND INFLUENCE PEOPLE

JOHN BLAKE

Published by John Blake Publishing Ltd, 3 Bramber Court,
2 Bramber Road, London W14 9PB, England

First published in the UK in hardback in 2002

ISBN 1 903402 76 X

British Library Cataloguing-in-Publication Data: A catalogue record for this book is
available from the British Library.

Design by ENVY
Typeset by t2

Printed in Great Britain by Creative Print and Design (Wales),
Ebbw Vale, Gwent

3 5 7 9 10 8 6 4 2

Papers used by John Blake Publishing Ltd are natural, recyclable products made from
wood grown in sustainable forests. The manufacturing processes conform to the
environmental regulations of the country of origin.

Every attempt has been made to contact the relevant copyright-holders, but some were
untraceable. We would be grateful if the relevant people could contact us.

CONTENTS

The story so far   v

1. One door shuts, another opens   1
2. Life in the Little Apple   9
3. The scorpion and the bullfrog   25
4. Behind bars in Van Demons' Land   37
5. The meaning of life   45
6. If she leaves me, can I come too?   55
7. The battle in the big court   59
8. Why Six-Toes gave up dancing   69
9. A Hitchhiker's guide to the gallows   81
10. Sword swallowers and double agents   87
11. The curse of the Bookie Robbery   99
12. Bobby Barron and the Bad Fairies   115
13. Rentakill takes redundancy   123
14. White slavers, skinheads and pinheads   133
15. Psychology of fear   149
16. Mad Micky   155
17. The right stuff   161
18. The tone-deaf kidnapper hits wrong note   167
19. The Prince of Pain   173
20. The Beach Ball didn't do it   179
21. Hopalong Tom   185
22. Renee, a hard act to copy   193
23. Who's who in blue   199
24. Who's who in the zoo II   215
25. Rematch: The courtroom diaries   241

About the Editors   259

THE CHOPPER

They fear him, they hate him and slander him with lies,
And keep wanting to try him on for size.
They offer him cash, sex and free beers,
All just to sweeten the bloke with no ears.
He carries two guns 'cos he knows it's smart,
One for the eyeball, one for the heart.
They pinched him on murder, and started to clap,
Then cried like babies when he beat the rap.
He's laughed at them all, since '69,
Knocked 'em all down, as they stood in a line.
But now he knows he's had his day,
And headed for Tassie – just walked away.

THE STORY
SO FAR

'I MIGHT BE A PSYCHOPATH, BUT I'M AN
HONEST PSYCHOPATH.'

MARK Brandon 'Chopper' Read was secretly released from Pentridge Prison on November 14, 1991, after serving nearly five years for shooting a drug dealer, criminal damage and arson.

Behind him was a total of more than 17 years in prison and a ghastly reputation for violence earned in a blood-spattered career as a streetfighter, standover man, gunman and underworld executioner. Ahead of him was an uncertain future.

Read is the son of a strict Seventh Day Adventist woman and a war-stressed former soldier who slept with a loaded gun at his side. His childhood was brutal, institutionalised and dislocated. As an infant he was placed in a babies home for many months before returning to his parents, who were later to separate.

Bullied and ridiculed at school because he was a slow learner and because of his mother's unusual religious convictions, the young Read responded first by impressing his peers with his tolerance of pain — and then with his willingness to inflict it on others. 'There are none so merciless as those who have been shown no mercy,' he was to note later, in an oblique reference to his strange and stressful childhood.

Read made up for his inadequacies by building an armoury of strengths. Naturally big and strong, he became ruthless, cunning and brave to the point of insanity. He carried a two-edged sword against the world: one edge was violence; the other was wit, and good humour, which he could use to conceal a conniving streak. Apart from his disturbed bloodlust, he was genuinely good company. Many police, prison officers — and those criminals who have not fallen victim to Read's violence — regard him as a likeable rogue. But those in the underworld whom Read has declared his enemies see him as a psychotic tormentor who will stop at nothing to win any battle he takes on.

Read has spent all his adult life involved in violence. He justified it by stating that he preyed only on other criminals and left ordinary citizens alone. He has been stabbed, shot, bashed and run over — but has survived.

A self-confessed killer and torturer feared throughout the underworld, Read made no excuses for his life. He still doesn't.

The first volume of Read's autobiography, *Chopper*, was published at the time of his release in late 1991. Based on more than 300 letters written from his cramped cell in Pentridge's maximum security H Division, the book gave a unique insight into the mind of a man who could take lives and laugh about it. The best-selling book turned the poorly-educated felon into a bizarre celebrity.

Read was filmed for US and local television, and excerpts of his book were syndicated in London's Fleet Street, New Zealand and every Australian state. But with his new-found fame came jealousy. Within months of starting a new life in Tasmania the dream started to sour. He was investigated by tax and social security departments after they were informed by unnamed 'sources' that the criminal turned author was getting huge royalties from his book. In fact, Read was struggling psychologically and financially to come to terms with being a free man. After half a lifetime behind bars, living on the outside was not as he had imagined. He continued to vow that he would go straight, but his associates in Tasmania included not only old mates but a new, dangerous breed — outlaw motorcycle gang members who shared Read's obsession with firearms. Soon, the grapevine was humming that Read was starting to take financial shortcuts and heading back to crime. At one stage it was rumoured he had returned to Melbourne and had been shot dead in Footscray in a gunbattle. Read was amused to hear the story while eating wiener schnitzel in a Launceston pub. But on May 14, 1992, he was charged with shooting one of his bikie mates, Sid Collins, with a 9mm Beretta pistol.

In spite of all Read had promised himself, his longtime girlfriend and police, he was back inside a cell just six months after his release. After a few heady months as an author and celebrity, he was now just another number in the Tasmanian prison system. He was convicted of the Collins shooting after two much-publicised trials: in the first the jury was dismissed after being unable to reach a verdict, and in the second the jury took three days to reach a majority verdict of guilty. Immediately, the Crown moved to have Read declared a dangerous offender, which would result in an indefinite sentence. On November 4, Mr Justice William Cox declared Read a dangerous criminal under Section 392 of the Tasmanian Criminal Code and ordered him to be detained at the Governor's Pleasure. He said that had the Crown not made the application, the sentence for the offence in other circumstances would have been six years. Read has appealed.

Read maintains his innocence. But, philosophically, he has

conceded there may be some rough justice because he has got away with so many acts of violence over the past 20 years. 'I could see the irony in finally going down on the one frigging shooting I didn't do after beating the system so many times before,' he noted after the trial.

Read began work on his second book even before his arrest — although, with typical audacity, he states that, 'like Oscar Wilde', he does his best work behind bars. Read's sequel takes the reader from the highs of gambling thousands at a legal casino to the lows of facing the rest of his life in jail. In between, he talks of his efforts to readjust to 'civilian' life — and reveals more of the crime stories that made his first book a national best-seller. A natural observer with an eye for detail, an ear for dialogue, a good memory and gallows humor, he gives an insider's account of the Australian underworld: fixing an unblinking gaze on the brutality, corruption and warped code of values of the criminal fraternity. He identifies some of Australia's high-profile criminals and police and pays them tribute — Chopper-style.

Even under the duress of standing trial for an offence that could ultimately send him to jail for life, Read produces from the dock a day-by-day account of the courtroom proceedings that are to decide his future.

Read's first book created a storm of controversy and, in some critics' minds, a moral dilemma. Why should a killer make money by boasting about the pain and suffering he has inflicted on other people?

Read's reply was brutally direct: 'No honest citizens hate me; they know I'm no threat to them. I don't prey on the weak and the defenceless. No one I have shot hasn't deserved it. My limp-wristed critics are really hypocrites. They don't really care for my victims.

They know the world is better off without drug dealers and other scum, but they want me either to shut up or cry crocodile tears ... which I won't. What do they care? I come from a different world and I make up the rules as I go along.

'For outsiders, it's like looking into a snake pit ... you don't really care which snake swallows the others. It just so happens that I'm the biggest snake ... with the biggest appetite.

'I find it the height of good humour that to some people my greatest crime is not so much killing and maiming the various drug dealers who have crossed my path, but that I refuse to apologise for it and wallow in some shonky show of public remorse in front of a TV camera.

'I might be a psychopath, but I'm an honest psychopath.'

The reaction to Read's first book was extraordinary. He received fan mail, offers for contract killings and requests for advice from people who wanted to murder their enemies. Total strangers visited him in jail asking him to sign copies of his book. Members of an occult group wanted to conscript him as a warlock. But the only offer he took up was to be the 'godfather' to a little girl whose mother has become a penfriend.

Despite his cult status Read remains a man without roots. With his 'kill-and-tell' memoirs he has distanced himself even further from the underworld but has also ensured that he will never be fully accepted in conventional society. He frightens both bad and good men. He is a man caught between the two worlds. To the civilised mainstream of society he is a monster. And in the underworld he is a failure who is feared, hated and can never be trusted.

Ultimately, criminals are judged not by their bravery or the scalps they collect but on their ability to make money and keep out of jail. By these criteria Read is a disaster. He suffers chronic injuries from being shot, stabbed, hit with a claw hammer and nearly kicked to death. Whether inside or out he will have to spend the rest of his life looking over his shoulder. He fears that his only claim to 'morality' — his virulent hatred of drugs — could be stripped from him. He confesses that he fears being set up with heroin so that he would be charged as a drug dealer. 'I would rather die than have that happen,' he writes.

And the future? For Read, it is bleak. When the doors of Pentridge opened that morning in November 1991, he was given another chance. In just six months he had botched it.

John Silvester and Andrew Rule

CHAPTER 1

ONE DOOR SHUTS, ANOTHER OPENS

'I PERSONALLY WOULDN'T HAVE
THE BAD MANNERS TO PUT ANYBODY
IN A BOOT — ALIVE.'

ITwas just after dawn on Thursday, November 14, 1991. The hatch on the cell door slid back. I could see the screw's face through the slit. I've seen better heads on a pig dog, but this time I could have kissed him. This was the morning I'd sweated on for more than four years. And, off and on, for 12 years before that. All up, I'd wasted more than 17 years staring at cell walls: dreaming about good times on the outside, brooding about the bad times inside ...

The door opened. The officer led the way through H Division, the toughest division of the toughest prison in Australia. Pentridge. The Bluestone College.

I stopped outside Franky Waghorn's cell and tapped on the door. 'I'm out. See ya, Franky,' I muttered. The big bald beach ball with the most dangerous pair of hands in captivity had been a good mate inside. But even he hadn't known I was leaving that day. News travels fast inside, and news like that could have made me very dead, indeed.

For the previous four months 'jail friends' had been showing an unhealthy interest in my departure date. Unhealthy for me, anyway, if certain parties on the outside had got wind of my movements.

The underworld is full of spies, and most of them are double agents. Mine had told me the Lygon Street Mafia had put the word out that they were very keen to know exactly when I'd be released. They are very formal types, these Italians, and I was a little concerned that they might want to give me a reception. But I considered I wasn't up to social engagements of this nature, as I felt I wasn't dressed for the occasion: I was wearing brand new blue jeans and a T-shirt as my going-away outfit, but I felt naked without a gun.

I knew I would be most vulnerable from the moment I walked out of the reinforced door of Pentridge until I walked through the pressurised one of a Boeing jet flying out of Melbourne. It would be the only time my enemies — and there were plenty — knew they could catch me unarmed.

One plastic 'godfather' who'd gone on an indefinite holiday overseas only weeks before had left instructions that I should be in the ground with a bag of lime before he came home. I hate to be a party pooper, but I intended to disappoint him. I still do. I've never liked the bloke.

I made two quick calls on my way out. One was to get a cab. The other was to my girlfriend, Margaret. I told her to put a few iceblocks into a bucket of scotch, because I was on my way.

Pentridge is like a little city, made up of self-contained suburbs; it's a long walk from the H Division cage to the front gate. When they finally opened the door I unconsciously flexed my wrists. It was the first time in nearly five years I'd been outside without wearing handcuffs. I was relieved that the taxi was waiting. I didn't want to hang around.

The driver looked in the rearview mirror, sneaking a look at me. I could tell he didn't like what he saw, but I couldn't blame him. After all, it's not every morning you pick up a 16-stone hitman covered in tattoos and with no ears.

'Where to?' he mumbled. 'The stock exchange,' I said. 'Where else?' I couldn't resist it. The bloke waited, and I killed off the joke. 'No, mate. Collingwood.' This time he believed me.

It was 7.02 am on the dashboard clock as the Falcon turned into Bell Street. I lit my first for the day. It was then I noticed the 'no-smoking' sign. Things had changed while I'd been inside. But the cabbie didn't say a thing. He was no fool.

We pulled up outside Margaret's joint. It was a $6 fare, but I handed the cabbie a tenner and told him to keep the change. I've always been a soft touch. Maybe it's a hangover from the days when I used to touch other people for five grand a week.

I went in. I gave Margaret a peck. This was not the time for any romantic routines — and besides, Margaret's brother Ronnie and uncle Charlie were part of the welcoming committee, and I'm an old-fashioned gent at heart. What she did give me was a huge glass of scotch, which I downed in two gulps,

It was 7.15. We had a chat and took a few photos. We sat at the kitchen table. It was surprising that after four and a half years on the inside, conversation didn't exactly flood out. There was so much to say, but it was hard to find the words. There would be plenty of time for sweet talk when we were safely off the mainland.

Ronnie, a loyal friend, was ready for the one-way trip to the airport. We jumped into his silver-blue Datsun 240Z. It was a good, fast car — but I didn't like it. It didn't have a boot. I am very partial to boots, as long as I don't have to get in them myself. I've only ever been in one, and that was enough.

I personally wouldn't have the bad manners to put anybody in a boot — alive, that is. It's far too uncomfortable for that.

Little Margaret was in the back seat. At five foot two she wasn't too cramped. By 8 o'clock we were heading north to Melbourne airport. It was a good run. The 'squareheads' were heading the other way towards town in their thousands, like lemmings The only nine to fiver I ever had was given to me by a smartarse judge for assault and battery.

It was an overcast but mild morning. As we slid past the factories I couldn't help thinking that it would be the last time I would see Melbourne alive. I made a silent vow that this was, at last, a fair dinkum new start. And that I'd only ever be coming back across Bass Strait in a body bag. My head was spinning. My brain was jammed with so many thoughts I got a headache. I was sad to be leaving the old hometown for good. I was delighted to be out of Pentridge and back with Margaret with our whole lives ahead of us. And I hated not having a shooter.

As Ronnie got up to speed on the freeway (making sure he didn't go over the 100kph limit) I adjusted the passenger side rearview mirror and kept watch. I was looking for wogs with bad attitudes — and I don't mean taxi-drivers who don't use their blinkers.

I knew I could trust Ronnie to back me. But guts without guns in my world can be fatal. I hadn't come this far to be a martyr to the mafia.

At the airport, we parked the car. There was plenty of time until the next plane to Tassie was due out. Too much time, I reckoned. I would rather have just jumped on a jet. I didn't have any luggage to check in: prison had nothing but bad memories for me, and I didn't bother with packing any mementos.

We had time to kill ... but after 17 years in the joint I was an expert. We headed to the bar. It was 8.55, far too early for a beer. I ordered bourbon and cokes all round. It didn't calm the butterflies in my guts, but it made them pretty happy.

I looked up on the departure board. Australian Airlines flight 539, Melbourne to Launceston, was boarding. There was no way on God's Earth I was going to miss this baby. We queued to board with businessmen and a few holidaymakers. Did I look out of place? I didn't give a shit. The ticket in my hand was my passport out of 20 years of violence, blood, grief and insanity. I had lost my closest mate, the best years of my life — and my ears.

As the big bird banked over Melbourne, I looked down and saw the tile roofs of Thomastown, where I'd lived most of my time as a kid. And I saw Pentridge, where I'd spent most of my life as an adult. It looked for all the world like an old-time fortified town, and it looked peaceful from up there in the sky. But I knew better. For me it would always be a cesspit of human vermin and weak-gutted mice. If I'd had a bomb to drop I could have done the world a big favour.

It was 10 o'clock when we landed. Back in H Division, Frankie and the crew would be doing the laundry. But I wasn't, and I never wanted to again.

We grabbed a cab and told the driver to take us to the North Lodge Hotel. And that was the last anyone saw of Margaret and me for a week. We had a lot of catching up to do ...

The only time we surfaced and left the hotel room was to go over to the park across the road. I thought about that park a lot when I was in jail the last time, because I had loved it when I was over in Tassie in 1987. I really hankered for its green open spaces and the ten friendly rock monkeys that live there. That's the modern world ... one short plane flight and you go from rock spiders in Pentridge to rock monkeys in Tassie. One nibbles nuts and the other ... forget it. Ha ha.

We moved pubs because it was far too expensive for an 'honest battler' like me. Now it was time to get on with life. We jumped into a taxi and headed out to see my dear old dad at Ravenswood. We pulled up outside the little unit, and Margaret went to the door while I hid around the corner.

I heard her knock on the door and introduce herself. Dad said, 'It's about time I had a chance to meet you, young lady.' She said, 'Well, I've got a bit of a surprise for you, too, Keith.'

Then I jumped out. The old bloke nearly fell over backwards. Then he jumped forward and grabbed me in a bear hug. He might be old, but he hasn't lost his strength. I hugged him back. We didn't say much. We didn't have to.

I was home. Later, I felt I should be put in one.

CHAPTER 2

LIFE IN THE LITTLE APPLE (OR WHAT I DID IN THE HOLIDAYS)

'PERHAPS THEY COULD CALL ME SAINT
CHOPPER OF THE PUMP ACTION.'

THE most frightening thing for me when I got out of jail in November 1991 was being sent shopping by Margaret with money and a neat little list, but no gun. Margaret didn't think it was manners to take guns to the supermarket.

When I was doing the shopping I would always suspect that some people were staring at me, and I wasn't being paranoid, as their eyes never seemed to leave me. I would dutifully get all the shopping on the list, plus about $100 worth of stuff we didn't need, only to be told off when I got home.

After I was on *A Current Affair* on television, I was walking through a supermarket with Margaret when one fat lady, standing with a bunch of other fat ladies and a flock of very ugly children, screamed out, 'Look, that's the man who was on the telly.' They all started to giggle and point me out. They started to chatter and carry on so I hid in the frozen food section until they lost interest.

At the checkout counter of another crowded shop I was saying,

'Yes please, I'll have one of those, thank you, it's a nice day, rah, rah rah' in my best, most polite going-shopping voice, when the woman standing next to me said to the sales girl, 'He's the most polite killer I have ever heard.'

I laughed along with them but, really, I was quite embarrassed. Some people would actually complain to the management that I was in the shop. What do they think I am, a vampire?

Then there were other people who would ask me to autograph a copy of the book while I was standing at the checkout counter. In the end I left the shopping to Margaret.

There is not a gunman alive who frightens me, but I became terrified of people in shops, especially of fat ladies in lambs' wool slippers. They would scream out, 'Look, that's the bloke on the telly. He's a murderer.'

Call me sensitive, but I couldn't cop that.

I HAVE a loyal and good friend who acted as a secret agent against a dangerous crew who wanted me dead. She risked her life for me and I will never forget her. Her name is Tracey Glenda Warren. She was the buxom young lady who acted as a double agent for me in matters of war with my enemy, the drug dealer Dennis Bruce Allen.

Tracey would cuddle up to Allen, but later tell me in detail the plans he had made for my death. It would drive him crazy that I always appeared to be one jump ahead of the psychotic little weed.

Now, there was nothing sexual between Tracey and me, although I have to admit that she was a top looker, with a 38-24-34 figure. I have many fond memories about Tracey, but that is exactly what I want them to be: memories.

Well, imagine my shock and horror when, two weeks after my release from Pentridge, she arrives on my dad's doorstep in Launceston.

I was with Margaret and my dad when a cab pulled up out the front at Ravenswood. We were having a quiet cup of tea when there was this enormous 'bang, bang' on the window. I nearly dropped my scone at the noise.

It was a screaming and crying Tracey yelling, 'Is that Margaret? I'll kill the bitch.' Now Tracey is a big girl, and she was hysterical. I had to physically restrain her from rushing through the flat door and engaging in mortal combat with Margaret.

But little Margaret is not to be trifled with. She was heading in the other direction towards the kitchen, no doubt looking for the carving knife. This could have been a real blood bath.

I had to pick Tracey up, and she is no lightweight, and carry her to a taxi rank. She was then driven off, not without a hail of verbal abuse at my good self.

Despite this dispute, I still have a soft spot for her.

Hey, women ... you can't live with them, you can't live without 'em. Pass the beer nuts.

I KNOW that the question of whether or not I really walked away from crime when I came to Tassie is on a lot of people's minds. I know that police and crims don't agree on many things but that many from both sides openly stated that I would be back in trouble sooner rather than later.

Well, I am the only man who knows what is in my heart and let me say that I have turned my back on the Melbourne crime world and I will never return there.

All I can do is put my best foot forward. But if, now and again, I put my best foot on the thick neck of some smartarse, that is not returning to crime, for God's sake.

But just because the lion has left the jungle, it doesn't mean that he automatically turns into a monkey. I am what I am and I am who I am and I cannot and will not change my mental and emotional makeup. Walking away hasn't meant that I have gone through a personality reconstruction. I have not become a born-again Christian, nor have I joined the Gay Liberation Movement. So when I came to Tassie I wasn't going to allow two-bob gangsters to kick sand in my face when I went to the beach.

I am not involved in crime or the criminal world. I have turned my back on my former life; however, I would relieve any man of his heart and lungs with a double-barrel shotgun if he tried to turn his hand against me or mine. In other words, hurt me or mine and I'll cut your ears off, put a hole in your manners and I'll rip your bloody nose off with a pair of multi-grips.

But the criminal world is no longer my business or concern, except in my new-found career as an observer and crime writer.

While some may think the pen is mightier than the sword, let me say that I will give up my gun when they pry it from my cold dead fingers. I will not eat humble pie or cop shit from others. Am I asking too much? I think not.

I was quite happy to be left alone. But I don't like being lied to, robbed or conned and I will not allow myself to be humiliated or belittled. Yes, I have walked away from it all and I will shoot any bastard who tries to drag me back into it.

I know it might sound a contradiction but while I look to the future my soul was tempered in the past.

I have not entered the priesthood, I have just turned my back on the Melbourne underworld, and that is all I ever set out to do. The people who are out to kill me, set me up, destroy me, betray me, lie about me and pull me down haven't gone away.

I had no illusions when I arrived here that my life would be trouble free. However, compared to my past life, I have been almost saint-like. Perhaps they could call me Saint Chopper of the Pump Action.

PS: Some uncharitable people might say my present legal difficulties arising from the shooting of Mr Sidney Collins prove that I have already returned to a life of crime. Not so. I am quite simply a victim of a case of mistaken identity.

ONE little giggle I had in Tassie was when I bumped into a Melbourne crim I had done time with in H Division. He was an Italian crook, kick boxer and drug dealer.

He wasn't hard to pick. There he was sipping a cold drink in my local, wearing slip-on shoes, an imported suit with hair gel by the bucket. He was in a pub with bikies and tough Tassie workers. Most of them still wear flares for the big night out.

I immediately wondered what this bloke was doing in the same pub that Margaret and I always attended for the big Sunday lunch.

He was here to buy guns, or so he said. I didn't believe a word of it. He was making too many phone calls for my liking.

We agreed to meet the next day. Naturally, I believed that he had come from the mainland on the instructions of some of the Lygon Street Mafia — the plastic godfathers who seemed convinced I would one day return to Melbourne to deflate their big fat bellies with a sharp instrument. These were the so-called heavies who slept with the lights on in case big bad Chopper ever decided to have a working holiday in Melbourne.

Anyway, to cut a long story short we drove our Italian visitor to the banks of the South Esk River. I then put my arm around him in an almost fatherly manner, and explained that the South Esk flowed all the way to the sea and that the current was swift.

I told him that if the fish did not eat the flesh from a body before it got to the sea, that the bloated dead remains would float into Bass Strait, never to be seen again.

He went quiet. This made me sad, as I hate to see a guest look unhappy.

Then I told him that there was a plane flying to Melbourne within the hour. I gave him an alternative. The river, or a few drinks in the airport lounge.

Frankie said he was thirsty. I wasn't surprised.

We drove to the airport. Frankie bought the drinks.

He must have had a pressing engagement he had forgotten about in Melbourne because he forgot to stop at his hotel to pick up his luggage.

Never mind. I am sure there are plenty of good tailors in Lygon Street.

Really, I was just having a giggle. But I don't think Frankie knew that.

ONE important matter that I should mention is money, or lack of it. I have written a book and people seem to think I walk about all day in a smoking jacket stuffed full of cash and live on champagne and caviar. In fact, people think I have become a millionaire through writing. Let me tell you I made more money with a blow torch than a ball point. And I didn't get too much out of the crime world either.

I have done most things in my life for a giggle, not for the money. But try to tell other people that. Government departments, legal aid offices — they all believe I am rolling in cash.

I have been told that because of the book, I will never get the dole, but what I have got from the book would not keep me in drinking money and ammo.

I have been told that I am supposed to have a secret bank account in Melbourne where there are millions stashed away. Well, I must have forgotten the branch account and the account number. Which is a pity, because I could do with a bit.

Sure, before Sid Collins was unfortunately shot, I had a fair amount of cash at one time and another, but most of that came from casino winnings, and it went back from where it came, with interest. It was fun while it lasted but it didn't last too long.

I knew that I would never get the dole while there was one copy of the book on sale. The employment market was not exactly crying out for out-of-work gunmen and toe cutters.

I am proud of the book, but it was no magic wand for making money, believe me. I also have been the subject of some TV interviews. I have found to my cost that TV people pay you in greasy smiles and flap doodle. So for those who think I have made a fortune out of making an idiot of myself on television, forget it.

While I certainly don't regret putting my life story on paper, the money earned is trivial compared to the massive headaches it has caused. Budding authors be warned: books are done for love, not lucre.

NOW, many of you will think that a respected (but mis-understood) literary figure like my good self would have plenty of common sense and brains. Sadly I appear to have gone out of my way to prove time and again that this is not so.

Once I got on the outside I thought the fresh air would clear away the cobwebs and that Margaret and I would live the quiet life.

I thought Tassie would be filled with wildlife I could hunt and fish I could catch. But there is something else down this way which lured me into deep water.

The casino.

It hooked me. Underneath it all I am just like most other blokes about. I like a bet, a drink, a good woman and the chance to occasionally catch some garlic-breathing, drug-dealing swine and take his loot. Pretty normal, I reckon.

So when I saw the casino it was as if all my Christmases had come at once. I would go there nearly every day. But I was no mug punter, not me. I developed a system.

My system was so good it enabled me to lose money at twice the rate of any normal tourist. Over an eight-day period playing my simple system of roulette I managed to have $23,000 pass through my hands. From one hand to the other and then back to the casino.

I blew $5,000 of my own dough in the process. That is $5,000 of legal money, not money from the old days. Once I would just shrug the shoulders, jump in the car and visit a drug dealer.

It would be a simple matter of explaining that my good luck was his good luck and my bad luck I would also share with him. Most would understand and hand over the cash, even before the blow torch flame went blue.

But I digress.

As an honest man $5,000 is a heap of readies. I would stay at the roulette table, sticking to my system and after a short time I could double, or triple my money.

Then I would get the fever, go crazy, and start to break my own system. I would bet in large amounts and then 'bing, bang, bongo' I would be broke.

I won $500 the first night, $5,500 the next night, lost the rest the following and so it went on. One night I was more than $7,000 up, then lost it in about ten minutes. I was getting into debt over gambling and that was crazy.

One night I was playing roulette at the casino and my luck was really in. Within three hours I had won $7,000. Within another hour I didn't have a cab fare. As I was about to leave the croupier who had spun the wheel and seen me lose a fortune said, 'Hey, Chopper, I knock off in ten minutes, can you hang about and sign your book for me?'

Bloody cheeky bastard. Nevertheless, I did hang about and sign it for him.

Margaret was furious and I finally snapped out of it. I would go up there with $100 or $200 and walk away. In all things the power to walk away at the right time separates victory from defeat.

When I left Melbourne and the life and death blood rush I lost something. It is hard to explain, but living on the razor's edge, with one foot in the grave, gives you a rush, just like a junkie gets from drugs. Why do you think people climb cliffs and bungy jump?

I suppose throwing money on a roulette wheel was a fool's way of getting a small rush. It was a small thrill, but it wasn't the same. I don't want to return to the old ways of crime but I must say that dicing with life and death did turn me on.

It is no use denying it, I got turned on living a life that would have frozen most men's hearts with blind fear.

WHEN I got to Tasmania and settled in it didn't take me long to run into a group of rogues, rednecks and renegades, who, like me, feel naked unless they have a gun in one hand and a stubbie in the other.

Many of them were former members of major motorcycle gangs. There was my now well-known former friend Sid Collins, a former president of the Outlaw Motorcycle gang, Black Uhlans Larry and Big Josh Burling, the president of the Tasmanian chapter of the Outlaws.

Now I have known bikers for 20 years and have always kept in close contact with one member of the Hell's Angels, known as 'The Lawyer' because of his great knowledge of matters legal and financial. I would often talk to him and he was able to set me right on who to trust in the bike world.

When I got out of jail and went to Tasmania I found that I was walking into all sorts of private bikie politics. In fact, I was asked to kill Sid Collins.

Here I was, out of jail for just two weeks and the word was about that I had come to Tasmania to do a hit on Mr Sid Collins.

Now, he was a rather formidable fellow in his own right so it was obvious I would have to settle this and quickly. I needed all this bullshit like a hole in the head and I knew that if I didn't settle it quickly someone was going to end up with a real hole in the head.

I was starting to wonder whether retirement in sleepy Tassie was worth the bother.

I went down there with the idea of getting a pipe and some slippers and enjoying the fresh air. But some of those leather-bound fatheads couldn't get it through their crash-helmeted skulls that I was an ex-headhunter. That I was not for hire, and didn't want a piece of their inter-gang rivalry.

I felt like Dame Nellie Melba (without ears) being asked to make a comeback. No, no, no, I would say. Yes, yes, yes, someone would reply. And besides, they never named a dessert after me.

I had only been out of jail six weeks and half the mad bikies of

Tassie seemed to hate me. Was it my aftershave, I asked. Now, I was used to the mafia and a few Melbourne drug dealers hating me, but this was going too far.

So I rang 'The Lawyer' in the Hell's Angels for advice. He told me the truth about some of the characters, including The Groper, Sid Collins and Black Larry.

I went out of my way to meet all of them to try and settle matters down. I told them that I had retired and had come to Tasmania to live the quiet life and not to take on any hits.

We had a million drinks and things seemed to settle down. At first I was treated with suspicion and distrust. But in the end, they seemed to accept me.

We formed the hole-in-the-head shooting club — a humorous, but clearly mental group with access to firepower which would put to shame the various crime groups and drug cartels from the mainland.

We would meet socially as many of us, sadly, did not have full-time jobs and we would decide it was time to have a meeting of this refined group of gentle sports shooters and gun aficionados. It was then time to fill the sky with lead.

After a few beers one day we were having a shot when a bullet ricocheted and hit one of the crew in the leg. No problems. We were able to dig it out and there was no harm done.

A LOT of people have asked me if I miss Melbourne. The night clubs, the wog shops, the card games, the massage parlours, escort agencies, the night life, the street life, the blood, the guts, the money and the excitement.

They ask me how I have settled into the quiet life of Tassie. People forget that 17½ years in Melbourne was spent in jail. The night life in Pentridge isn't too lively, believe me. Watching cockroaches run up the wall is not a big night out.

The point is that I am a gun freak and, for me, Tassie is heaven. I have fitted in well here as a responsible member of the Tasmanian community. I love shooting and hunting, blowing the heads off native wildlife like the locals. Ha, ha.

Your average gun-toting Sydney or Melbourne crook couldn't hit the side of a barn with a shovel full of wheat whereas I could blow your nose off at 100 paces.

As for night life, forget the disco scene. I prefer to walk through the bush with a sporting model .303 and a bottle of whisky and a lackey carrying the spotlight. That is all the nightlife I need.

Of course, I also like to go to the casino and play roulette when I'm not hunting. Screw Melbourne, a city of plastic gangsters, smacked-out whores and bad shots.

I love Tassie.

BUT I'm now sad to say that the hole-in-the-head shooting club is no more. Whoever fired the shot in the chest of Sid Collins fired the shot that finished the shooting club.

Trent Anthony was put under police protection after the shooting, along with the Ford Fairlane I gave him as a gift. Another member is hiding under his bed while his wife cruises around Launceston in the car I gave him as a gift.

The rest of the crew seem to have made up their minds about my guilt and don't want to know me.

Of course, Big Josh Burling, Mad Micky and Mad Mike have stuck by me. The Sid Collins shooting has taught me a thing or two about the guts and dash of the rogues of Tassie. It doesn't exist.

How did I get involved with them? I can't even ride a scooter without falling off. Whenever I foolishly allow myself to trust I am betrayed. Perhaps I will have to become a hermit to be safe.

SINCE I have been in Tassie, I have been approached by many and various odd-bods, who have read the first book and feel that they are free to approach me on all matters of violence.

I am constantly amazed at how blood thirsty the average member of the public really is. I have been approached in relation to killing this one and that one.

There seems to be a never ending stream of people out there who would like to see their next door neighbours, hairdressers, doctors, accountants, wives and husbands knocked off.

As a retired member of the crime world I treat these discussions of murder and contracts as the height of good humour. But many of these people are serious. Deadly serious.

One day a very old timber man, a wood cutter of the old school, approached me and asked whether I would be interested in killing the Tasmanian independent 'Green' politician, Dr Bob Brown.

He said he would show me where he lives. He said Dr Brown had a place in the bush where I could pick him off easily.

I was polite and respectful to the man. After all, he was nearly 80, and it would not be polite to laugh off the offer of a political assassination. So I asked him, 'What sort of money are we talking?' He said, 'I'll pass the hat amongst the boys. I think I could get $500, which is nothing to sneeze at.' Pretty bloody small hat, that's all I can say.

The sad thing was, the old boy was serious, bless his heart.

NEVER SAY NEVER

Never say never again,
Even when the sun shines,
You know it has to rain,
We all try and fly straight,
We all want to love,
None of us want to hate,
But shit happens and things change,
You might have to pull the gun,
When trouble comes into range,
But night after night and day after day,
You see trouble and you try and walk away,
But you can only walk 'till your back's to the wall, Then someone has to
live and someone has to fall.

CHAPTER 3

THE SCORPION AND THE BULLFROG

'IT NOW APPEARS TO ME THAT I CAN ONLY
TRUST SOMEONE WHEN I HAVE A LOADED
GUN STUCK IN THEIR MOUTH.'

IT took Read exactly six months and 450 kilometres to turn the full circle. He was back in a prison cell charged with the attempted murder of his friend Sid Collins, the former Melbourne president of the Outlaw motorcycle gang. As Collins lay near death in the Launceston General Hospital Read was enjoying his continuing love affair with the gaming tables at the nearby casino.

Around midnight on 13 May Read was leaving the casino in a taxi when he was surrounded by ten police, all with guns drawn. He was ordered out of the cab. Read responded, 'What's this? A tax assessment?'

Read's dry humour fell on deaf ears, for his driver and mascot Trent Anthony had already made a statement identifying Read as the shooter. Strangely, Collins himself originally stated that he was shot by an unknown man outside his house in High Street, Evandale.

Days after Read was charged, Collins changed his story. He said he had been sitting in the back seat of Read's Ford sedan when the former Melbourne hitman turned from the front passenger seat and shot him in the chest.

The charge of attempted murder was later dropped to grievous bodily harm. Police alleged Read shot Collins in the car and that Anthony and Read then drove the badly wounded man to hospital. The weapon, a .9mm Beretta pistol, was later found hidden in the backyard of Read's home.

Collins later claimed that just before the shooting Read had said to him: 'Do you want one in the brains?'

The bullet entered Collin's chest, deflected off a rib and passed through his colon and — according to medical evidence — damaged one kidney 'like taking the top off a boiled egg'.

Read had been close to Collins and claimed he had paid for the ex-bikie's fiancée's wedding dress. Just before the wedding Read wrote to Collins from Risdon Jail, 'Dear Sid, I regret to inform you that I will be unable to attend your forthcoming wedding celebrations due to pending legal matters. Wishing you a speedy recovery. Regards, Mark.'

MANY years ago the old former boxer, merchant sailor and standover man Vincent Villeroy told me he thought I would die in jail or on the gallows. I was highly offended and asked him why, and he just replied, 'Because, young fella, that's just the way you are. A man is what he is and all the preachers, school teachers and the best-laid plans in the world won't change what you are.'

Then Vincent told me a story I still remember 15 years later ...

The scorpion and the bullfrog were on their way home and both came to the edge of a raging river. The scorpion couldn't swim, but the big bullfrog was a powerful swimmer. The scorpion said: 'Let me climb on your back and you can swim me across the river.' The bullfrog replied, 'You must think I'm stupid; if I let you ride on my back, you will sting me and I will die.'

'Don't be silly,' said the scorpion, 'if I sting you we will both drown.'

The bullfrog thought about it for a moment and then replied, 'Yes, of course, I see your point. OK, you can ride on my back.'

So the scorpion hopped aboard the frog's back and the bullfrog started to swim powerfully across the flooded river. But as the bullfrog reached the middle the scorpion lashed out with its poisonous tail.

The frog cried out, as the venom began to paralyse its hind legs, 'Why, why, why now? Now we will both drown.'

'Why?' said the scorpion as it was swept away to its death. 'Because that's just the way I am.'

That old story is coming back to haunt me now. For years I refused to believe it, but a man who won't face reality is a fool, so I must face it.

I have tried so hard to change, to leave the sordid life I have lived, to turn over a new leaf, but shit happens. And I always end up cold as a stone in a cell only fit for an animal. The result always seems to be the same.

If my life is worth anything it is as an example to others of what not to do and how not to live. There is no glory in crime, just blood, tears and misery.

Some people look up to me. I think they are fools, but they can go home to their warm beds and their families and I am left in hell.

In spite of my smiling face and outwardly happy nature I have cried a sea of tears. The only reason I don't commit suicide is that it would please too many arseholes.

But I often ask myself, why do I bother?

A YOUNG crim in Risdon Prison said to me, 'Chopper, you're a living legend.' I thought about that. Yes, I thought, I'm a 'living legend' who blew every penny at the racetrack and casino and gave it away to sob stories and hard luck tales. I'm a living legend who, after 17 years in jail, got out and together with the woman he loved, set himself up in a beautiful home full of lovely furniture and things, a large legal gun collection, two cars, a driver, a bodyguard, friends, parties, barbecues, clubs, pubs, racetracks and casinos, fine food and booze.

My life was looking a million dollars. I may not have had a million dollars — but I lived like a millionaire. All I did when I went out was shake people's hands and sign people's books. And, yet, here I sit once more in a prison cell, my life in tatters, and Margaret back in Melbourne.

In a blood and guts gang war, gun-in-hand situation, I've been called a criminal genius. However, in normal living of day-to-day life outside, living like normal people live, I am a social retard. And in money matters I'm a total fool.

It broke my heart to see Margaret walk out of the prison gate in tears. She loves me. But after ten years she couldn't — and I wouldn't want her to — go through this bullshit again. That's why I pleaded not guilty on the charge of attempted murder. However, win, lose or draw, I am guilty of putting myself in a foolish and stupid position, which has put me back inside a prison cell. After a lifetime of reading men and studying tactics and strategy, I fell victim to the 'smiling face' routine myself — and trusted false, fairweather friends. What a fool I am.

To anybody young or silly enough to think otherwise, the criminal world is a not a wonderful fairytale world of money and magic. It is not populated by a fine, fair-minded body of men. And while I may offend the feelings of some so-called friends and so-called experts, they should know that what I have revealed about the underworld has come from the heart. You can fool some of the people some of time, but in the long run people won't keep spending money on a book that talks shit. And like it or not, for better or worse, I don't talk shit.

Here I sit in Risdon Prison, Tasmania, otherwise known as the 'Pink Palace', facing many more years in jail.

I can't be trusted with money. I either spend it, gamble it or give it away to others, as I am a natural sucker for a sob story. I did try, but it seems that in spite of my best efforts my life is what it is and I am who I am, and whether I am innocent or guilty I can't seem to wash the blood from my hands ...

As Oscar Wilde lay dying, a priest asked him, 'Do you renounce Satan?' Wilde replied, 'I hardly think this is the time to be making enemies.'

I don't know why that thought about Wilde came to me, other than he did some of his best work while in prison, spent a fortune while he was alive yet died a pauper. But don't forget, the opera ain't over 'til the fat lady sings.

As I have maintained from the beginning in this shooting case, it was a set-up. Not the police, mind you. Too many people owed me big money, and I was a bloody easy mark — a scapegoat.

The fact that the gun was found hidden under a log in my back yard three days after the shooting — when all I had to do, if I knew it was there, was to tell Margaret to toss it in the river — proves it was a set-up. After all, I spoke to Margaret five times between the time of the shooting and the time they found the gun.

I am naturally shocked at Trent and the victim, Sid. However, people continue to shock us all the time, don't they?

I'm starting to wonder if I will spend the next 20 years of my life being dobbed in, loaded up and set up for this, that and the other by various nitwits who see me as the perfect scapegoat. Tasmanian police only have to hear my name mentioned and I feel they suspect the worst. I was told by a Tasmanian detective that my name gets mentioned in police stations regularly by individuals who have been arrested, and who then try to offer various wild stories in relation to Chopper Read to try and lighten their own load.

The Tasmanian police force is not Scotland Yard, by a long chalk.

There is a small-town mentality running through Tasmanian thinking — and a naive logic. If the 'smoking gun' is found in your letterbox then you must be guilty. I'm sure it's because of the book that they brought in the heavyweight himself, the Director of Public Prosecutions, Mr Damian Bugg, to do the prosecuting on a grievous bodily harm charge.

About two months after I was arrested for the shooting of my former friend Sidney Collins, a local chap by the name of Ronald Jarvis went missing, believed murdered.

A month later the police arrived at Risdon Jail to interview me in relation to the Jarvis matter. Police had been given information that I was either behind the Jarvis incident, had ordered it done or knew the people involved.

I'd never heard of the fellow. Dropping my name in police stations over various crimes has become a statewide pastime.

When a Launceston man was beaten with a baseball bat and relieved of $6,000, I was under suspicion. Just because the guy was a suspected drug dealer, I was the bloke in the frame. When another so-called toughie was seen with facial scars and a badly cut face, it was rumoured that I had pistol-whipped him. Launceston is a large country town and so is Hobart. Rumours, gossip and whispers have become a way of life here.

On May 14, 1992, Police seized from Read's Launceston home a cache of arms. They took a Ruger 10-shot .22 carbine, a Savage .22 bolt action rifle, a Stirling .22 bolt action, a Sportco .22 bolt action, a .303 rifle, a Stirling .22, an Ace .22, a Baikal .22, a Boito single-barrel, sawn-off 12-gauge shotgun, assorted ammunition, two rifle scopes, a pair of nunchakus and a revolver shoulder holster.

WHILE on the subject of how I have been treated down here, it's interesting to look at the property seizure receipt which lists the weapons taken from my home in Launceston after I was arrested.

Apart from my Ruger carbine and Mark III .303 they only listed the lightweight weapons I used as wall decorations.

It seems this bloody Sid Collins fiasco has cost me a lot. The amount of guns I have lost over my lifetime would arm a small military unit. It's a crying bloody shame.

I have plenty more guns, but I did love the particular range of weapons taken, and I feel quite sad at their loss. I wonder if they will ever be returned.

You can have nothing in your wallet, and nothing in the bank, but if you don't own a gun, you're really broke. Take my money, take my wife, you may even try to take my life — but leave my guns alone.

On my solid brass belt buckle there are the words: 'I will give up my gun when they pry it from my cold, dead fingers.'

IT seems to me that my whole life has been a battle, fighting the never ending forces that pit themselves against me. A good fight is a delight, I just love to wage war. A mental and physical battle against a worthy foe is all part of the great chess match of life.

The sad thing is the betrayals that you face along the way. You may place so much faith in someone, only for them to let you down when you need them most.

People just don't stay the same; they can change sides, turn under pressure and go where they think the strength is.

My good friend Cracker Phillips left my side because he felt it was the wise thing to do. I am still godfather to his eldest son, Jarrod Brandon Phillips. The old hole-in-the-head shooting club is split into two.

How did it happen? My refusal to kill one man saw another man shot. I left jail and came to Tasmania to leave a life of violence and now I have a new flock of enemies.

I must now face it that this is my lot in life. Mahatma Gandhi I ain't. Any rate, I'd look pretty silly walking into a pub dressed in a towel. Where would I hide the gun?

I walked away from crime in Melbourne because I wanted a peaceful life. Now I wonder what I have walked into.

'Let me have men about me who are fat, sleek headed men, such as sleep at night. Yon Cassius has a lean and hungry look, he thinks too much, such men are dangerous.' This is a verse from Shakespeare's *Julius Caesar*, and where does it leave me?

The only friend I have who is fat and bald is Frankie Waghorn, and he's in jail.

I have always found it hard to trust people. The correct selection of a friend is a difficult task. I mean, what is a true test of friendship? Shoot them a few times in the arse and see if they remain solid or tell on you would seem to be fair, but I suspect you would run out of friends before you ran out of bullets.

My old mentor, gunman and hard man, Horatio Morris, once said to me, 'Young fella, never grow to love anyone too much, because you never know, one day, you may have to kill them.'

Those words once chilled me to the bone, but as I get older, I am haunted by them. It now appears to me that I can only trust someone when I have a loaded gun stuck in their mouth.

It seems to me that every time I drop my guard with people and try to relax it all goes wrong. As soon as I place faith in someone or believe in their word of honour, I get dumped on.

Face to face, people seem to be as good as gold, but once I walk away and leave them to it, I get betrayed, lied to, conned and robbed.

While there are a few exceptions to the rule, it seems that I will have to travel through life with the cynical attitude that all the people I come in contact with are traitors waiting to happen.

How can you find if females will stay loyal? I know about Margaret — she has stood blood loyal through everything that has happened, but it is very difficult to judge some women.

Sex is not a test. I have known some women who would go to bed with a German Shepherd if he had cash, took her to dinner and barked sweet nothings in her ear.

And most men would betray their own grannies to save their own stringy necks.

It is the ultimate battle, to know who to trust and who to watch. The words of an old Sicilian bandit still haunt me, 'My enemies I fear not, but heaven protect me from my friends.'

I lost a few so-called mates after the first book because they got upset about things I wrote, or felt that I didn't give them glowing-enough mentions, which surprises me as I would have thought half of them couldn't read anyway.

It has been an interesting exercise as I have learnt a lot about some of the people I thought would remain staunch to me. I have been the victim of acts of treachery and betrayal that have astounded me, but many of the old crew have remained loyal and stay in touch.

Joe 'The Boss' Ditroia still writes from his cell in Adelaide, the Hoddle Street killer, Julian Knight, writes to my dad and, of course, Craig 'Slim' Minogue and Frankie Waghorn stay as solid as ever. Frankie's mother is a sweet old dear. I envy Frankie having such a lovely mum.

There are others on the outside who have been loyal. Dave The Jew, of course, Billy 'The Texan' Longley, Bobby Lochrie, Sammy Hutchinson and Mad Micky Marlow have all stuck.

There are too many to call, but I must mention my lovely lawyer, Anita Betts, who has done the right thing for me. Margaret, who has been through so much, has remained loyal and I will always remain in her debt.

It seems that a bloke like me brings the worst out in human nature. People are either really bad to me or show me great kindness. I guess that despite all the treachery, life's not that bad really.

CRIMINALS who do not use drugs and do not deal in them are considered to be straight criminals involved in straight crime.

I am one of the few who can stand up and say that I am an old-fashioned crook who has steered well away from selling drugs. I have always had the paranoid fear that I would one day be set up by my many and various enemies, or even some police who might like to see me out of the way.

All they would have to do would be plant drugs in my car or home, or get some stupid junkie who was desperate to get out of trouble to invent a story and give evidence against me.

I have never had the hint of drugs or drug charges against me and I am very proud of that. I am totally clean in that area and for a crim to say that after 20 years in the underworld is a proud boast indeed.

It is a fear that I have that, instead of trying to kill me, they will try to set me up. I would rather be set up and shot than set up with a drug charge.

Am I paranoid? I don't know. It stands to reason that sooner or later my enemies will consider this. Let me put it another way. If I was Chopper Read's blood enemy, that's how I would do it.

SENSE OF HUMOUR

The mail came today,
One letter had a lot to say,
Tearful crying across the page,
A message of puzzled rage,
What, where, how and why,
Great concern that he would die,
Asking me if I was the offender,
Or the victim of a false pretender.
An angry young lady writing a letter,
It seems someone got hit with a 9mm Beretta.
I never replied. What's to be said?
No sense of humour, nobody's dead.

CHAPTER 4

BEHIND BARS IN VAN DEMONS' LAND

'A BLOKE WITH NO EARS HARDLY EVER GETS
A SECOND LOOK DOWN HERE.'

I HAVE spent about 20 years in different Victorian prisons and boys' homes and I thought I had a fair idea of how jails worked — and don't work — but things in Tassie are different, let me tell you.

The oddest thing about Risdon Jail is that it's a little bit like a boy scout jamboree. They don't have Divisions, they have Yards. I have spent my time in the Remand Yard, or H Yard. The child killers, sex offenders, police informers and protection cases are kept in E Yard. But here is the giggle ... E Yard has a footy team and they play the rest of the jail.

These vermin walk freely in the jail without any fear of violence. Why? Because, if you can believe it, it is against the rules. If one of these human mice is hurt on the football field the other prisoners say, 'Come on, play fair.' There is not a great deal of dash shown by the inmates of Risdon Jail. No wonder it's known as the 'Pink Palace'.

There would be about 250 inmates in the Tasmanian prison

system and about 220 of them are assorted dogs, hillbilly retards and child sex offenders. There would be about 30 solid crims in the system and about that many on the outside.

But I suppose the same can be said about crims on the mainland. I feel that win, lose or draw, someone like me is out of place wherever I go.

ONE bloke in here had a very attractive girlfriend. When the Navy arrived in town she couldn't keep her pants on. She was keen to show some Tassie goodwill to our brave fighting boys. So, the Tassie boyfriend broke her leg and said, 'Go on, hop down to the docks now and have a good time.'

I nearly fell over when he told me that his grandfather used to wander about a little so they would tie his leg to a 20ft length of rope attached to the cherry tree so he wouldn't get lost.

Another bloke here lived in a town that had two pubs and he was barred from both. When Margaret and I met him he was standing outside one of the pubs asking people going in if they would mind buying him a stubbie and bringing it out for him.

When he wanted a counter meal he would write out an order on a bit of paper and would send in the order and his money with a passerby. They would then serve him his meal on a table, outside the pub. No one minded serving him food and grog, as long as he didn't come inside.

Sometimes he would wait an hour until someone passed the pub who would get him a drink. Poor bugger: only two pubs and barred from both.

Some blokes in Tassie are as tough as anything you'll find on the mainland. One of them, Spratty, a former SAS veteran from Vietnam, who now works in the timber industry, hit himself in the head with his own chainsaw and lived to tell the story. Another bloke cut his thumbs off for the accident insurance. It leaves me in the shade, I can tell you ... a bloke with no ears hardly gets a second look down here.

One half-mad bastard left his young child on the edge of the washing machine, when he came back he found the child had fallen in and drowned. Two days later his second child died of cot death. His father gave him the money for two headstones for two little graves. He thanked his dad and then blew the money at a greyhound meeting.

In its own way, Tassie is a hard state with hard men, and I don't mind the place. But as far as the local crim population is concerned, they have never been taught correct underworld etiquette.

The average Tasmanian involved in crime simply cannot be trusted inside a police station. They seem to leave their guts at the front door and turn into crying little schoolgirls.

I have been told by the senior prison officers here that they know I am writing a book and they are not happy.

It would appear they want to sabotage my literary efforts. I am amazed that they are so opposed to good writing. One would have thought it was a better way to pass the time than indulging in violence or helping others making escape plans.

As I sit here in cell 27 I can hear another inmate singing, 'On top of old smoky, all covered in red, one in the heart and one in the head.'

The same guy made up a song for me.

'Chopper went to Risdon in the year of '92.
They had him on a charge he really didn't do.
And when he gets out,
He'll find the lying dogs all gone,

North, to the mainland,
North, the rush is on.'

I AM sitting here in my cell in Risdon writing a letter to Margaret, when a light bulb falls out of the ceiling and hits me on the head. I don't know if I should take it as an omen of some sort. It has never happened to me in jail before.

Risdon Prison, the big boys' home, is the coldest prison south of the equator. But apart from the cold, it is totally harmless. If I go back to crime, it will be somewhere warm where at least I can work on my tan.

I have taught the boys in the remand yard the song, 'I don't care if it rains or freezes, as long as I've got my plastic Jesus on the dashboard of my car.'

The police have taken my whole gun collection. I am heart-broken. That leaves me with a mere 30 guns hidden away that they didn't get. I will be unable to defend myself, ha ha.

I am afraid that guns have always been my weakness. I still have a collection buried in Melbourne. Four Eskies wrapped in chamois leather and gun oil. I may lose the argument, but I will never lose the war.

ONE prisoner here at Risdon is a minister of religion who knows my dad and has been very kind to me. He is doing time for receiving stolen goods and tickling the offering plate. He swore that the stolen television sets found in the back of his church in Launceston were gifts to the church, but the court disagreed. He is a grumpy old coot but he keeps me supplied in smokes and chocolates.

Another character here is the disgraced accountant, Colin Room, the fellow who refused parole because of work commitments inside the prison. He is a happy and bright personality who flutters around the prison, busily managing the affairs of the jail. He is involved in everything from the budget of the canteen to the debating team's programme.

Colin is another mate of Mad Micky Marlow. He is a likeable enough fellow who is always smiling. If I had his money, I'd be smiling too. He is not any sort of real criminal, more a colourful character with a taste for creative book-keeping. Some like him got invited to the Lodge; he just got invited to the slammer.

Colin is writing a book on the 'history of Tasmania'. I am sure there will be an overwhelming demand for a book on the history of Tasmania. Ha ha, I am sure it will sell well.

RAY Sheehan is an old-time bank robber, payroll bandit and general 'stick 'em up merchant'. He is from the old school, one of the dying breed who don't believe in giving people up in a police station.

I have known Ray for 20 years. He is now in his 50s and doing it easy here in Risdon Jail. It is like a little retirement village for Melbourne crims. Ray was originally a Tassie boy who went to Melbourne to do some robberies. But when he returned to the state of his birth — yes, you guessed it — he succumbed to the temptation to do another stick-up. The bloke is totally hopeless.

I am sure that, in time to come, news reports will tell of a 100-year-old man with a gun in one hand and a walking stick in the other, hobbling off down the road after robbing a bank. When they catch him, his name will be Ray Sheehan. He may not be Jockey Smith, Mad Dog Cox or Ray Chuck, and he never will be, but one thing is for sure, the old boy's done more stick-ups than Ned Kelly.

ON September 24 the boredom of Risdon Prison life was broken when I was told I had a visitor. I don't get many visits here so I went up to find a bloke I had never seen before. He was a young man named Mark, which isn't a bad name, at that. He told me he was from South Australia and was in Tassie on his honeymoon. He told me that he and his young bride were having a wonderful time in Tassie. Then he produced a copy of my first book from under his arm and asked if I minded autographing it for his brother.

Now this was not the Myer book department and we weren't at some literary lunch, but the screws said they didn't mind, so I autographed it. The visit lasted only about five minutes and then he was on his way, happy with the world.

He left me standing there, totally amazed. The screws were a bit shocked as well. I wouldn't mind if I could find another 11 like that. They would make a great jury.

THE BALLAD OF RISDON JAIL

So here I sit,
So here I dwell,
Yet again I sit,
In a prison cell.
Harsh, cold, cruel and callous,
The jail they call the Pink Palace,
It's not the prison that makes me sad,
My life is a prison of its own,
As for the Palace, what can I say,
Freezing, bloody cold, night and day,
The wind, the rain, the frost and hail,
That's the ballad of Risdon Jail.

CHAPTER 5

THE MEANING OF LIFE, WITH REMISSIONS FOR GOOD BEHAVIOUR

'I SERIOUSLY CONSIDERED KILLING MY OWN DAD AND BURYING HIS BODY.'

ONE of my favorite songs is 'The Great Pretender' by The Platters. As far as emotions and emotional matters are concerned, I guess I do pretend to a great extent.

Not many people will believe this, particularly those that I have bashed, or had their feet warmed with the gas blowtorch, but I don't feel hate. I just don't know what it feels like. I mean, I can pretend to hate, but the most I can feel is to be a little cross with someone.

Love is another emotion I can't really understand, or truly feel. While I say that I love this one or that one, it isn't an emotion that truly touches my soul.

'Love' and 'hate' are words I simply use, because they are words that I have been taught to use like lots of others. My violence, even taking a life, has nothing to do with hate. Business is business and that is what it is for me.

Love? Well, I love Margaret and I love my dog, the famous Mr Nibbles. I love my dear old dad and I have loved various friends, but it is an emotion I can't come to terms with. I guess if I trust someone, then I love that person, and I trust dear little Margaret most of all.

The doctors have called my feelings in relation to love psychopathic, but I don't know so much about that. Doctors seem to have a tag or a label for us all.

I do know that I pretend to have feelings and emotions that other people seem to have. For example, I have no real sense of fear, not because I am truly brave, but I simply can't see the danger. Fear is just a word to me. Hunger and thirst I can feel, but hate and love I can only imagine.

I can get an angry feeling when someone has offended against me and a warm kind of feeling towards a person who has shown me warmth and kindness. I think many people are confused about love.

I never loved or felt love for my mother. After all, I was in a home as a baby, and if you haven't felt that emotion as a child, it is a bit late to try and develop it, or grow it, in later life.

I know that little Margaret loves me, and I know that I can trust her, but I know that I am a bit of an emotional mystery to her, as I am to myself. Feelings are things that I have to pretend to feel in order to be seen as normal by other, so-called normal people.

When I kill someone, I feel nothing except 'I hope no one is watching', and that isn't an emotion, it is a concern. In other circumstances, I feel lust. But that isn't an emotion; it is a physical feeling.

I think I am a very empty person inside as I don't seem to be able to feel all these normal things that others say they feel. I can really like someone or something, or I can really dislike someone or something, but that is a little different to hate and love.

Once in the 1970s during one of my many battles my dad was threatened by my enemies. The threat was worse than death; it was that they would put him in a wheelchair.

I seriously considered killing my own dad and burying his body. I had two reasons. I didn't want my enemies to have a victory over me and also I felt I could do it quickly and painlessly, thus saving the old fellow any suffering. I guess in a way that is a kind of love, isn't it?

I still use the words love and hate, but that is because I can't find other words to express what I am feeling. I am a pretender. Trust is the most important thing to have, and if I can say to myself that I trust a person, then, in my own way, I love that person.

The whole emotional question is a bloody confusing mystery to me. The older I get, the less I feel inside about anything or anyone. I know some fantastic people, who I trust and who are loyal to me and who I would kill for without a blink of an eye. I have enemies who will be my enemies until either they or I die.

But true love and hate, what is it all about? I really don't know. These are matters I don't think about much, because when I do I get confused. As you can see, psychopaths aren't meant to feel anything. But as you can see, I feel a great many things. My only problem is that I don't know what I am feeling.

Well, dear reader, that is a small insight into the inner mind and heart of Mark Brandon Read, leaving you with the question: is he the sanest man in the world, or mad as a hatter? Personally, I have no idea. After all, what's mad and what's sane? Life is like a merry-go-round, so instead of asking what and why, we should just enjoy the ride, because thinking too much can strain the brain.

Questioning every element of life is man's greatest curse. So much for the heavy-thinking Chopper. For goodness sake, pass the Panadol, I have a headache. Mark Brandon Read, the thinking man's psychopath.

Some men ask why. Some ask why not. I say, bugger it all, who gives a shit. Play on, the umpy hasn't blown the whistle.

Yet.

WHILE I have never tried to blame anyone for the way my life has gone, I have always skipped over my childhood and the horrors of my early days.

Many crooks lie on their shrink's couch and cry about their past. They love to blame others for what they have become.

I am the first to say that I am what I am. But I would be stupid to suggest that my past did not help contribute to what I have become.

My childhood helped for the attitudes and opinions that I now hold. So, without pointing the finger of blame I will say that I am, in part, a product of my past. We are all victims of what we have been through.

So, to all the parents of the world, remember you may be responsible for moulding the next great world leader, or the next mass killer. Be careful, it is in your hands.

A child's mother and father can be the salvation or destruction of the youngster. The American mass murderer David 'Son of Sam' Berkowitz had such a lovely mother. And, yes, so did Chopper Read. When a child is driven to thoughts of killing his mother, he may grow up to kill his brother many times over.

MY little sister Debbie wrote to tell me that I am not welcome in her home because I am a sinner and a murderer. Thank goodness that's all she was worried about ... I thought it may have been because I had poor table manners.

Religion has been the curse of our family for generations, and Debbie has inherited her share, and mine too, from our strict Seventh Day Adventist mother. But what these 'true believers' forget is that more people have died and have been murdered in the name of religion than anything else. Even Jesus Christ was murdered, nailed to the cross, because of religion.

Nothing much hurts me, but to be called a murderer by my own sister and to be barred from her home hits pretty hard. I will never be able to see my young niece and nephews. That hurts me more than I can say.

I have never considered myself a murderer. I've put a few bastards off, but so what. Since when has swatting flies been murder?

People must know that taking a human life is a contradiction. If you kill 10 men you are a bloody murderer, but if you kill 10,000 you are a politician. That is Irish logic if I have ever heard it.

POPULARITY seems to be the pot of gold many people spend their whole lives searching for. I have never bothered to try and look for popularity. Being hated, being unpopular, is safer ground. If you seek popularity, you will generally fail, ending up a pathetic figure of scorn and ridicule. You can even destroy yourself in the process. But men who are hated can actually gain a following of loyal admirers, while some who seek popularity end up being disliked and hated. These are people who won't stand up for what they believe in, but act only to be liked by others. People end up seeing through them.

It is a confusing psychological topic. It is strange because I have received mail from people who reckon I'm great, because I'm the biggest arsehole they have ever heard of. So you figure it out.

I KNOW that in reading what I have written people could become confused, because they don't understand the rules under which I live. That is perfectly understandable, because there aren't any. There is no real black and white, no 100 per cent right and wrong. Good and evil can be very confusing. Everything in life, including most people, is built on contradictions.

I haven't written a book to get people to understand Mark Brandon Read. I mean, who really cares? The book is a look inside a dirty world most of you have never seen, will never see and wouldn't want to see close-up.

Maybe it is a little bit of peek-a-boo into my mind and heart. If it is, then it is only a brief glimpse. But people should also look at themselves. Everyone interprets what is right and wrong, good and evil in their own way.

The criminal and the honest man have fought each other since the beginning of time. Some say that good always wins but evil is not truly beaten. Does one side need the other? Does one man need the other? I sometimes wonder myself.

If bastards and bad men are so hated, why do good men love to read about them?

People love to watch movies about bad guys. They are fascinated by the other side. Is it a mirror of themselves? This is certainly heavy thinking. I must stop it before I get a headache.

We are all in search of the Holy Grail, the ultimate truth, the meaning of life. If God came down to earth and we all sat at his feet and asked, 'Lord, tell us the answer,' he would say, 'Piss off, I'm trying to find where I came from.'

So why bother searching. Don't worry, be happy. It is a good story, so read it, and don't worry about what makes the author tick.

After all I don't know. Why should you?

I KNOW I am hated in the criminal world, and seen by many criminals as some kind of psychotic monster, a freak.

I have never been accepted as a member of the mainstream

criminal culture, nor would I want to be. I have always been considered to be some kind of vulture, a shark in a tank filled with guppies. A mental case psychopath who doesn't follow their rules, but makes them up as he goes along.

I am, or was, a headhunter, and a lot of what they say is true. But to the criminal world, that is what I will always remain. I am rejected by them through fear and that is the way I want it.

But the straight world is filled with squareheads who are frightened of me. They have no idea how to talk to me and few, if any of them, have any idea how to approach me or treat me. And few, if any, relish the idea of mixing with me socially. So I am an outcast from both worlds. I am not welcome on either side of the fence. I am left in limbo, a creature from neither world. I am neither wanted nor trusted.

I have friends in the criminal world and friends who are honest, but most of the people who have stuck with me are social outcasts like myself.

It is little wonder that even though I have given crime away, I always have to be on guard. I am ill at ease, and can never really relax. I guess that is my lot in life. I am my own creation, and now I have to wear it.

It is difficult to live, knowing that most people see you as a freak, but that is the way it is.

One thing I want to make very clear, as a criminal I am in a class that is no threat whatsoever to Mr and Mrs Average. The normal honest person has nothing to fear from me. Chopper Read won't break into your home, he won't pinch your TV, video or purse. He won't rape your daughter, wife, sister or granny. He won't pinch your car, rob your bank, café or off-licence.

No, I am not in an area of crime which would personally touch

bove: The hole in the head shooting club … (left to right) Sid Collins, Me, Cracker
hillips and Junior Westbrook. Sid was later to form a splinter group, the hole in the
ts faction. Ha ha.

elow. Trent Anthony, who was later to give evidence against me, draws a bead
ring target practice.

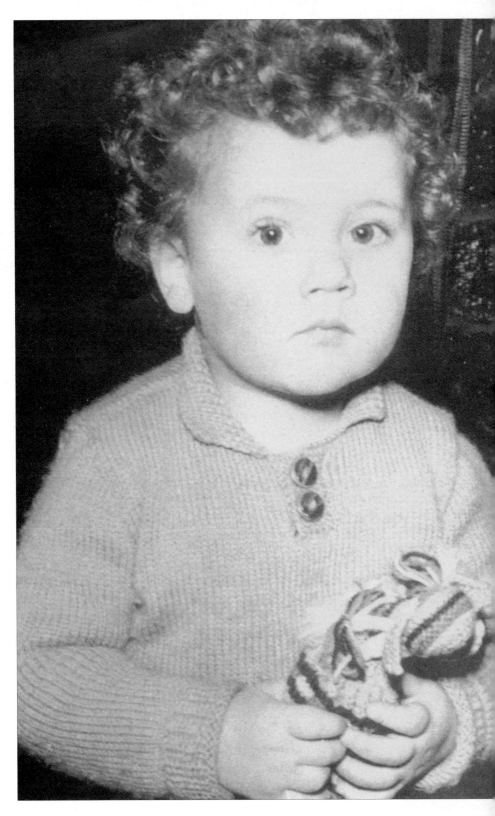

The Nipper who became …

... the Chopper.

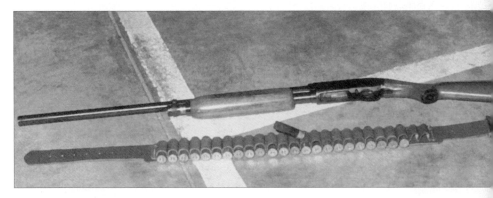

Above: The .357 magnum found in the boot of my car.

Middle left: The Beretta pistol found in my backyard.

Middle right: Another .357 magnum police found at Sid's house.

Below: The pump action shotgun found in the back of the car

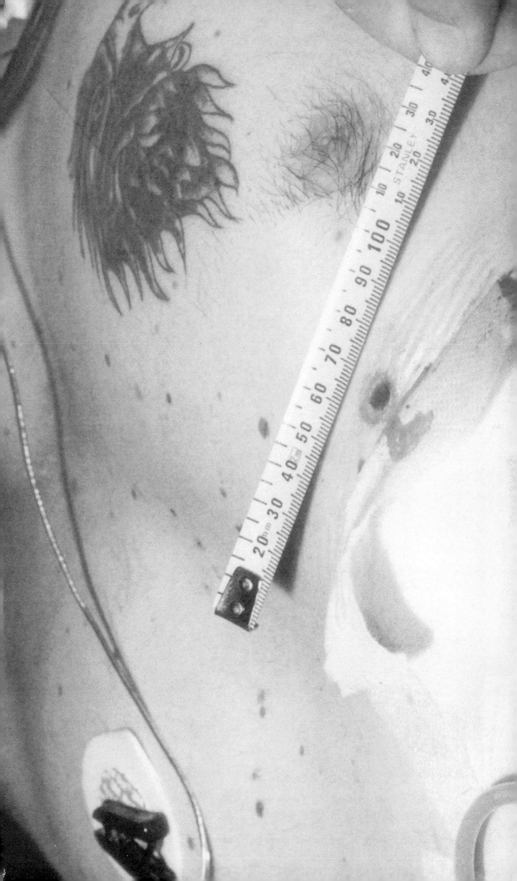

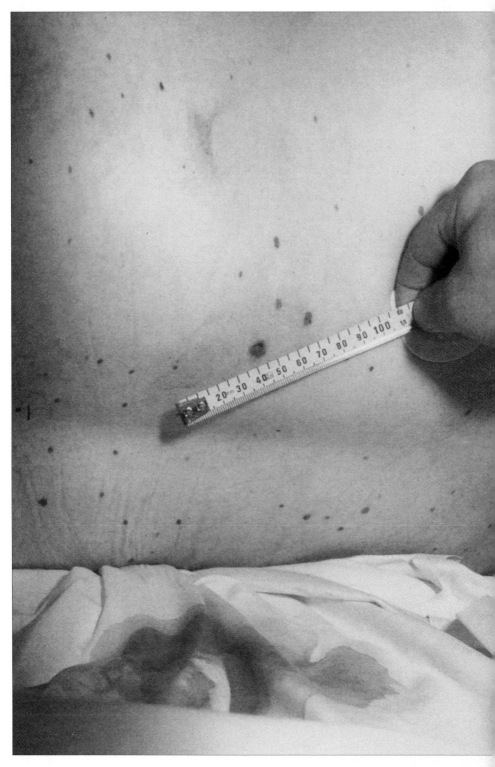

Previous page: Acupuncture, Tassie-style … the entry wound in Sid's chest. I have always found hairy nipples most unattractive.

Above: The exit wounds in Sid's back. Such a big fuss over such a little hole.

bove: Mad Micky Marlow and his very good friend Kelli. I sincerely hope she hasn't got an itchy trigger finger. And (*below*) I do wish Karen would make her bed.

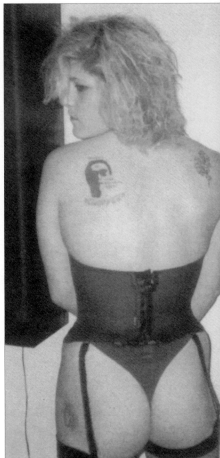

Top right: Karen, the 'White Dove', a local Launceston lass showing off her tattoo of the Aussie version of my book. Thank goodness she didn't take a fancy to the Encyclopaedia Britannica.

Top left: Self-proclaimed president of the Chopper Read fan club, Jackie from Queensland, wearing her badge of office.

Bottom right: Tracey ... my double agent in Melbourne, but not welcome in Tassie.

the lives of the ordinary individual. I am not even in an area of crime that will touch the ordinary criminal. I am, or was, in a league alone, working in a specialised area of crime that the ordinary type of criminal only comes into contact with in his worst nightmares. I must say that I no longer even enter that world. I am out of it, and no longer a threat to anybody.

Admittedly, I am still a violent person — but only if pushed. And the normal straight person will not push me, so where is the threat?

I was the rattlesnake that ate the spiders and left the wood ducks and rabbits alone.

In Australia I am seen as a bloody monster but in Northern Ireland they have been doing it for years.

I AM aware that a great many people have a love-hate relationship when my name is mentioned. Some love me, bless their twisted hearts, and a great many more hate me.

But the fact remains, that in the criminal history of Australia, 100 years from now, three names will stand out as unique characters: Ned Kelly, Squizzy Taylor and that mad bastard with no ears Chopper Read.

When Mark Brandon Read is dead he will still be the topic of bar room conversation long after the names of his enemies are long forgotten. In a world as ego-driven as the criminal scene, that is no small boast. As possibly the biggest egomaniac in the underworld, I think that is quite funny.

If everyone who hates me was to buy a copy of this book, I could die a wealthy man. If that isn't the last laugh, then I don't know what is.

TO quote the Irish comedian, Dave Allen, 'As I was going up the stair, I met a man who was not there, he was not there again today, I wish that man would go away.'

I am constantly meeting men who are not there. I guess all men at times show one face in public and another face in private. Weak men pretend to be strong, cowards pretend to be brave, losers pretend to be winners, perverts pretend to be normal, mad men pretend to be sane, criminals pretend to be honest, and liars pretend to be truthful.

Junkies pretend that they don't have a problem and whores pretend to be good girls. For better or for worse most people have two sides, the side they show and the side they hide.

But there are other people where what you see is what you get. Funny, isn't it, that the up-front person is generally criticised. I've never been two-faced. If I had two faces, I'd certainly wear the other one. At least then I would have a pair of ears.

CHAPTER 6

IF SHE LEAVES ME, CAN I COME TOO?

'IF ONLY I WAS NORMAL, SHE WOULDN'T
HAVE TO GO THROUGH HELL.'

MARGARET and I have been together for ten years, if you can call it that. She is a widow without a body to mourn over. Most of the time I have known her I have been on the inside.

But when we have been on the outside we have had a great time together. I simply wouldn't toss that aside for the sake of shooting some ratbag, then driving him to hospital, then hiding the gun in my own backyard.

She is still with me in spirit, still sticking with me through all this heartbreak.

We've had a few tiffs. In fact, we had one big blue over my gambling. She threatened to leave. She ranted and raved and threw a few punches at me. I threatened to leave. She said, 'You don't have to leave me. I'll leave you.'

But I walked over and started to take the guns off the wall. When she saw that she knew I was serious. She started to cry and said, 'If you leave, can I come too?'

I love her, but I can't understand why she still loves me.

After all those years of waiting for me, Margaret is still loyal and still in love. Don't ask me why. I would have left Chopper Read years ago. I still don't know what it is that Margaret sees in me, or why she loves me, or what makes her stand by me through the fires of my insane life.

She is tougher, stronger, harder and more solid than I ever will be. She was in her early 20s when we met, now she is 'thirtysomething' and more rock solid loyal than ever before.

Margaret grows stronger, not weaker, as she gets older, and she seems to get better looking as the years pass.

I believe that I am a lucky bloke to have known her at all, let alone have her by my side. In return, all I have ever given her is pain. Margaret is a mystery to me. I have said it a thousand times before. Thanks, Bubbie, I love you.

I am a tough bloke, but when I saw her leaving Risdon Jail to go home to Melbourne with tears in her eyes, I felt broken-hearted. If only I was normal, she wouldn't have to go through hell.

CHAPTER 7

THE BATTLE IN
THE BIG COURT

'I KNOW MY NOT GUILTY PLEA IS A FART IN
THE FACE OF A THUNDERSTORM.'

AFTER Read's arrest Tasmanian police became concerned for the safety of some witnesses connected with the prosecution case. They received intelligence that one of Read's closest friends, a mysterious, mentally-disturbed hitman known as 'Dave the Jew', was on his way from Melbourne to even the score. Both Trent Anthony and Sid Collins were placed under guard. It might have been a wise move.

I AM my own worst enemy.

I will fight to win this case, but I must face the fact that I haven't a leg to stand on with the weight of evidence I now face.

If a man says he was shot and he says that I shot him, then that's it for me.

I know my not guilty plea is a fart in the face of a thunderstorm. Even my friends and loved ones secretly believe I must be guilty because I have been guilty so many times before. Most of my life I have been guilty of something.

It feels so out of place and abnormal for me to tell friends that I really didn't do it. They agree with me and say, 'Of course you didn't, Chopper, we believe you.' Then they give me a funny look or exchange glances which tell me they think I have been up to my old tricks.

However, I march on in the face of it all. Don't ask me why.

SOME of my so-called friends have deserted me. But it was good to know that some people like Mad Micky and Dave the Jew, would always be there for me.

As soon as he heard about this spot of bother Dave flew over to see the Apple Isle. Now, I know The Jew means well, but with me on the inside and him on the outside, anything could happen.

I don't want this little bit of fuss to get out of hand and I don't need assorted people going on the missing list. Win, lose or draw, I have to live in Tassie and it is too small for Melbourne-style blood wars. I explained this to Dave over the phone and he agreed, although he argued that one or two wouldn't hurt.

I just said, 'Dave, please go home,' and he did. But first he saw Margaret and our dog, Mr Nibbles, on to the ship and safely back to the mainland.

Dave's loyalty to me over the years has been very touching. Most of my so-called friends here have lost their dash, except for characters like big Josh Burling.

TWO weeks before the shooting I was approached by someone in the bikie world in Tasmania with an offer to kill another man. I was told that I would be paid $10,000 for the job, but it was to be on credit.

I roared laughing: I wouldn't shoot the neighbour's dog on the nod. But once I refused the offer, the attitude towards me by some people changed dramatically. I don't know why, but I was treated as an object of suspicion. Perhaps those who wanted me to kill thought I may tell the other side. Then there is a shooting and I am arrested. It is a mystery.

I am supposed to have wanted Collins dead. Well, then, why isn't he? Sid Collins was driven to hospital at 100 miles an hour, enough to blow the welsh plugs out of the motor of a hotted-up 1974 Ford Fairmont. This proves there was no attempt to kill him.

I am a crack shot. I can shoot a stubbie of beer out of a man's hand at 20 paces. Sid was shot at point blank range, so why wasn't he shot in the head? If I had shot him, I could have taken his eye out at ten paces.

The gun involved was conveniently found under a log in my backyard three days later. The .410 sawn-off shotgun I used to kill Sammy the Turk in 1987 is still missing. None of it fits.

MY lawyer is Anita Betts, a sharp-minded, good-looking little honey. As lawyers go, I have never had a better one, and I have had some top lawyers in my time.

Anita has the competitive spirit to try to win. She throws the polite legal niceties out the window if she feels her client is not getting a fair go. She won't try and sell you out or do deals with the Crown behind your back. She is cunning and hard working.

I have never been so impressed with a lawyer. She is a legal streetfighter with a great set of legs. The prosecution seems to hate her, and with good reason. She is on the way up.

EVEN though we are now on different sides of the courtroom, I feel that is not a reason to lose one's manners. After all, I was invited to Sid Collins's wedding. I even lent him the money for his fiancée's wedding dress. So the other day I wrote to him and said, 'Dear Sid, I regret to inform you that I fear that I will be unable to attend your forthcoming wedding celebrations due to pending legal matters. Wishing you a speedy recovery. Regards, Mark Brandon Read.'

Sid Collins and Simone Watson were married on July 18, 1992, and about 50 people attended the reception. Sadly, I was unable to attend as I was in Risdon at the time. However, I was informed that a number of high-spirited revellers went to the Launceston Casino and were heard to make a number of loud and drunken threats against my good self.

I reckon that if that's the way they feel then Collins should give evidence which would result in my acquittal so they can kill me on my release.

It doesn't matter if I am in Melbourne or Launceston, the same sort of drunken and drug-crazed threats are made against me by weak-gutted mice. It seems to me that this verbal, 'we hate Chopper' vomit is only voiced when I am safely behind bars.

When I get out, or look like getting out, the same thing will happen. Mouths will shut and holidays will be taken. These mice are so predictable. I find it sad that this sort of crap should start against me in sleepy old Tassie.

I believe that Sid Collins was shot as part of some motorcycle club rivalry. It is a puzzle to me, but I do not see why I should be blamed for the puzzle. Some of the thinking in the criminal world would be the equal of the KGB and the CIA on a big day.

NOW, in matters of crime and violence I can be a touch naive, but even so, I am a little confused on the Sid Collins matter. You see, Mr Collins is a former president of the Outlaws Motorcycle Gang. I have watched the old Jack Nicholson movies and I always thought that big tough bikers stuck to the code of silence in matters of violence.

Why, then, has Sid turned Crown witness against me? It is all most odd. As he is a former President of the Outlaws, it casts a shadow over their good name. Even stranger is the conduct of another former friend, another president of a biker group who has threatened my life, foolish fellow. He is acting as a bodyguard for Sid.

It seems strange that other bikers would protect a man who has so clearly broken the rules of the club. What the hell are these so-called heavy men so worried about?

I believe the man who really shot Collins is someone in the bike world. Blaming me is the easy way out. We may never know the truth about the shooting. I know that Sid's attitude to me changed about two weeks before the shooting.

Whether the shot was fired within my car, I really don't know. For some odd reason, the police did not fingerprint the inside of the car, even though it was the crime scene.

Finding the 9mm Beretta in my backyard was a lovely touch. I know the police didn't put it there. I have no idea why Sid blamed me for the shooting. All I know is that the Crown evidence doesn't add up. I believe the true story of the shooting is more unbelievable than what has been revealed in court.

I am not Simpson with his donkey. I don't take wounded men to hospital. I don't even take dead men to the morgue.

IT is sad but true that there aren't many tough guys left. Money, drugs and good living has weakened so many. Few of them can sit in a police station and face the prospect of losing their toys and their treasure.

The 'code of silence' these days means 'whisper, whisper, but we want our names protected. We want to be kept out of it'. So as long as face can be maintained and the tough guy solid image can be kept intact, then 90 per cent of the so-called tough guys these days will spill their guts in a police station.

The moral fabric of the criminal world is a memory. Hard men are a dying breed. I live in hope that we can turn back the clock, but we won't. Criminals today and the world they live in is as weak as jelly. So why are the police still losing the war?

Because you can't clean up a sea of vomit with a mop and a leaky bucket.

The police finding the Beretta in my backyard is almost laughable. In reality this is a two-bob shooting matter, an attempted murder charge dropped to grievous bodily harm, yet they are treating it as if it was a double murder.

ANITA came to visit in me at Risdon for our last legal conference before the battle. She was wearing a pair of gold stiletto shoes and white cotton, stretch pants. She is definitely the sexiest lawyer I have ever had. As she sat opposite me patiently explaining courtroom tactics and strategy, I am afraid I completely last the plot.

It is difficult to concentrate one's mind on matters at hand when one is harbouring highly illegal thoughts about one's lawyer.

We must look a puzzling sight as we go to court; the Beauty and the Beast factor must come into it.

I have had some top lawyers in my time: Aaron Schwartz, Colin Lovitt QC, Boris Kayser and Pat Harvey. But believe me, Anita Betts is hot stuff. She is bloody magic, and for a bloke like me, a good lawyer means everything.

I AM used to having a few people in the crime world show me a bit of grudging respect, but I was very surprised to find a couple of Tasmania's finest were on my side.

While I was waiting for the jury to come back from the first trial I was surprised to see a very attractive policewoman and her young male partner come down to my cell in the Supreme Court.

They said they wanted to shake my hand, as they had read and enjoyed the first book. I must be the only crim in Australia with a police fan club.

WELL, it was a hung jury. All I needed was three out of the 12 to feel that there was reasonable doubt and I had the hung jury. It has to be a unanimous verdict, 12 out of 12, within the first two hours and it can be a majority verdict of 11 or ten after that. But if ten can't agree it is a hung jury. That meant that I only had to sway three of them and she's a hung jury. A second hung jury and I walk out the bloody door.

When I gave evidence I was able to tear the Crown case to shreds. To be honest, I didn't have a shred of evidence my way. They pulled in 30 Crown witnesses, including two so-called eye witnesses.

All I had was logic, and an 'It doesn't add up' argument. The Crown even had the cheek to quote part of my book to me in front of the jury. 'Bullshit baffles brains,' I said. 'You are quoting a few sentences to me out of a whole book. Allow the jury to read the book and they will understand my meaning.'

But the Crown would not allow this. The only witness for the defence was my good self. Anita Betts performed magically. I do love a good courtroom battle and some of this has been the height of good humour.

A second hung jury and I will walk free. All is not lost.

ANITA

Do you need a little aid?
After a night out with the blade,
Or put a bullet in a heart,
And need to talk to someone smart,
Got pinched having fun
With a high-powered gun?
Then get yourself a lawyer, son,
She's the tops and she's legal,
And attacks like an eagle,
But you'll never get one sweeter
Than the lawyer named Anita.

CHAPTER 8

WHY SIX-TOES GAVE UP DANCING

'HE LOOKED QUITE SURPRISED WHEN I
PULLED OUT MY TRUSTY MEAT CLEAVER AND
SLAMMED IT DOWN ON THE BAR, REMOVING
HIS FOUR FINGERS AT THE KNUCKLE.'

READ's spirits improved after the jury in his first trial failed to reach a verdict in August 1992. But Margaret had returned to the mainland and, while eagerly anticipating the second legal battle for his future, he was back in all-too-familiar surrounds. He could not start another prison 'war', as the other inmates either liked him or were frightened of him. So Read took up what he does second best: writing about crime. For him, it runs close behind the real thing: committing it.

IN the 1970s a young Chinese chap hanged himself in Pentridge. Me and Mad Charlie were standing over some of the inmates in the boys' yard so we were questioned over it for some reason. Obviously some cynics felt there may have been some foul play. Nonsense, the boy was in a strange country and probably felt homesick.

We were just teenagers at the time but we were moved from the boys' yard after the suicide and went to the Remand Yard.

It was around that time that a child sex killer was in the jail. He was an animal. The word in the jail was that he had raped and murdered a young girl in a particularly sickening manner. This fellow was on strict protection at the time in an observation cell.

He was taken for a shower once a day and locked back up so that no one could get to him. Half the jail wanted to kill him and he knew it. Some thought it would only be a matter of time. It is very hard to protect a man 24 hours a day, no matter how hard you try.

The little observation cell the childkiller was in had two doors fitted to the doorway. The main one was solid steel, the second was a steel grille which could be seen through. The main door would be left open so he could get some air, but the second would be locked so that we couldn't get to him.

We would spit at him and try to hit him with jugs of boiling water, but he was a quick little deviant, so we hardly ever got him. The screws — most of whom were fathers — hated him as much as we did.

Everything comes to those who wait ... and one thing about jail is that there is plenty of time to wait. One day the grille door was accidentally left open. The prisoner was heard to yell, 'Sir, Sir, please lock my grille gate, quickly.' He was in a panic, and no wonder. The screw he wanted must have been on a tea break and obviously couldn't hear him. Pity.

When the prison officer came back, the inmate in question was hanging by the neck, dead, with piss dripping down his leg from wetting himself.

I think in all the rush we forgot to tell the prison officer that the gate was left open. It didn't matter. The murderer must have been very depressed and couldn't live with his foul crime, so he apparently took his own life.

No big deal. But some inmates and staff had the bad taste to suggest that it was a set-up and that someone had let me out of the Remand Yard at the very time the grille was open and that my good self and another had strung the poor soul up.

Naturally I dismiss such stories as foul slander and gossip. Some inmates with too much time on their hands would believe anything they heard.

ONE of my mad mates in Tassie is a bloke I will call the 'Penguin', and not because of any similarity to the cute fairy type that toddle up the beach at Phillip Island in front of busloads of Jap tourists. The Penguin is not cute, definitely not a fairy and would bite a Jap on sight if he got half a chance.

The Penguin is a bit of a strange one. Recently, he was charged with some trivial matter like creating a public mischief or some such nonsense. When asked by the beak if he had anything to say before sentence was passed, he said he suffered from a multiple personality disorder and the doctors had told him that he had as many as seven different personalities. The magistrate, who must have been in good humour, replied, 'Multiple personalities: well, I sentence you to seven days' jail, but the rest of you can go free.'

It was all very funny in court, but it's no joke for the poor old Penguin. I have seen him walk up to the bar at a pub and order seven beers: one for him and six for the other blokes living inside his head. It's not a cheap shout, being a psycho.

The Penguin is ex-army, and has been a fisherman, waterside worker and slaughterman. He is no longer welcome at the Royal Derwent Mental Hospital and he has been in and out of Risdon Jail like a yo-yo.

He is a lovable maniac, as a lot of madmen tend to be. He has the reputation as a bad bastard, earning himself a feared reputation as a bar-room brawler who loves blood and guts; in other words, an all round type of fellow and not a bad bloke at all.

And despite his own problems, he finds time to take an interest in social issues and natural justice.

There was a case not so long ago concerning a 'rock spider', a child sex offender, who took a nosedive off the Tasman bridge into the drink. It wasn't the fall that killed him; it was the sudden stop at the bottom.

Now, some unkind people have had the bad manners to suggest that the Penguin put a sawn-off shotgun to the rock spider's head and gave him the choice of either taking a dive, or having his brains blown out.

The rock spider elected to take the dive.

The Penguin naturally dismisses such statements as foul gossip and rumour.

YES, I am a violent crook and yes, some of my critics at literary lunches have accused me of being a psychopath, but while I am at home with a blowtorch or a sawn-off shotgun, even I have my limits.

I must tell you of a little Maltese chap who played the system something fierce. While I was working up an honest sweat torturing drug dealers to make a living, this bloke would sit back getting regular cheques from the government for next to nothing.

Now I was responsible for getting this guy the easy life but what was in it for old Chopper? Not even a thankyou card or a Christmas present.

The man involved was a chap I will call Maltese Joe. He worked in the sheet metal industry but when he didn't work he was involved in gambling at various card games around Richmond and Prahran.

While he loved to play cards, this bloke obviously wasn't the full deck himself as on one occasion he attacked me in a hotel in South Yarra with a broken bottle. This was neither healthy nor polite. Luckily I managed to ward off this nutty little Malteser with a pool cue.

He ran off from the hotel threatening me with death, telling everyone he was off home to get a gun.

Maltese Joe's girlfriend worked at another South Yarra pub and in jest I had said to this woman, 'Darling, you would have to be the ugliest barmaid I've ever seen.'

I was a bit pissed, and I shouldn't have said it but, dear me, she was a total pig dog. But with certain people of ethnic persuasion, truth is not a defence and the Maltese bloke vowed that no matter how long it would take, he would get me.

Well, I walked into a pub in Windsor and he was standing at the bar, one hand on a beer and the other resting on the bar. He looked quite surprised when I pulled out my trusty meat cleaver and slammed it down on the bar, removing his four fingers at the knuckle. I then walked out.

Eighteen months later I found that Maltese Joe collected a large, five-figure workers' compensation payout and a pension for life for losing his fingers, apparently due to an accident at work on night shift at the factory.

How he worked that one out I'll never know. I suppose he had the last laugh, and not even a drink in it for old Chop Chop. Even though he was less than generous in sharing his good fortune with me, it would still be wrong for me to put the finger on him. In polite society, it's simply not done.

IN my first book I explained that I have been in love for years with the most wonderful woman in Australia, the publishing mogul and thinking man's thex thymbol, Ita Buttrose.

As the world now knows I had the words, 'I LOVE ITA BUTTROSE' tattooed on my bum. I had this done as my own personal tribute to a wonderful woman.

It is now criminal folklore that a group of us in H Division in the early 1970s formed the Ita Buttrose fan club, because in those days, the only magazines we were allowed in the top security area were the *Reader's Digest* and *Women's Weekly*.

I have told the story of how a drunken fool, now known as 'One-eyed Pauly', bad-mouthed Ita in an inner-city pub while I was standing next to him. Needless to say, I could not just stand there and allow the sainted Ita to be defamed in such a foul way without me leaping to her defence.

It was a short but vicious fight which I managed to win. In the book I described how when he was out cold I made sure he lost an eye. But there was more to that fight than you, dear readers, were told. Imagine my surprise when I read the published version of the book to see that I had been cruelly, and in my view unnecessarily, censored from telling the full story. Now all can be revealed.

It seemed that some people thought the true story was a touch distasteful, and should not be told in full. Needless to say I disagree most strongly.

What really happened that day was that there were some very tough men in that pub, many of whom were friends of Pauly. So when I got him on the ground my troubles weren't necessarily over. I looked at the man on the ground and I looked at the mob around me, and the thought struck me I had better do something to show that his mates should keep out of it, then and forever.

I bent down and, quick as lightning, popped his eye out and

dropped it in a glass of beer. I then drank the lot in front of the crowd. Pauly's mates all went different shades of green but it didn't seem to worry him, as he was out cold.

I didn't feel guilty about it, after all Pauly was left with one perfectly good eye, more than enough for him. He was a violent and bloody criminal who had spilt more than his fair share of innocent blood over the years — so please, don't feel sorry for him.

In fact, I recall the incident with some fondness, because I believe that the swallowing of an eye was a first in the annals of blood and guts brawling in Australia.

OK, it's not exactly like climbing Everest, but it is a record of some sort. I remember downing the beer in two gulps. The eye went down like a bantam's egg. I didn't blink, and neither did it.

After all, it is quite socially acceptable to have a snack with one's pre-dinner drinks.

To me violence was an art, and I was the artist.

THIS is a story I was never going to tell. It explains why I have such a deep-seated hatred of the parasites who sell drugs.

The truth is I have a real fear of putting needles in my arm because I myself was the victim of a set-up which very nearly killed me. Apart from the time when I was abducted at gunpoint and forced to dig my own grave, and when I had my guts carved open in Pentridge by Jimmy Loughnan, it's probably the closest I have come to death. And I'll never forget it . . . or forgive the treacherous vermin that betrayed me.

Years ago, during a very low time in my life at H Division, I was depressed and not in a well state of mind. It was then that I was talked into trying heroin by a few of the boys in the division.

They were all telling me it was great and would help me through my troubles. How was I to know that it was a plot to kill me. They put a full gram of heroin into a spoon, plus some acid out of the H Division fire extinguisher, mixed it up and filled the needle. I held out my arm, and the deadly mixture went into my blood. But, for some unknown reason, I survived. I was big, I was strong and lucky. And I sometimes wonder if Somebody up there was looking after me, because I have had more than my fair share of escapes from death.

Afterwards, they called me 'Rasputin the mad monk' behind my back. Mad is right. When I recovered, I was as mad as a cut tiger snake, and I handed out punishment in no uncertain terms. But I was so ashamed of myself for being such a stupid fool that I vowed to punish drug dealers whenever I had the chance. I now distrust and despise drugs and the scum involved.

If I had wished at any time in the last 20 years to go into the heroin trade I could have done so very easily. I know who to call, who to speak to, who to rob and who to kill. I could fly to Melbourne and lay my hands on two to four kilos of Chinese White with little or no fuss. Maybe one or two men shot, but no real damage done. I then could have that bagged up into one-ounce lots. I could make a million bucks in a month. And I could kill or cripple anyone who threatened my trade. No one who knows me doubts that.

If I wanted to go into the amphetamine trade, I could fly to Melbourne and rob a factory with no great trouble. The same with grass. I could march a major grower out to his crop and cut 30 pounds of top head worth about $6,000 a pound. I never had the wealth of my enemies, but that was my personal choice. If I wanted to go in that direction I would have made Mr Asia look like a street dealer.

But to be a drug dealer? Where is the honour? Where is the pride? Where is the personal respect? Even a man with no friends and family has to look himself in the mirror. At least I can do that.

I climbed up the blood and guts ladder of the criminal world, by the force of my own hand, not the coward's way up, using white powder and black money.

I'd hate anyone to think that my problem with drug dealers has ever been jealousy or envy. It's just that I despise them. They have no right to wealth or power.

SIX-TOES Ray Read, no relation, was not a criminal. But maybe he should have been. He choked to death on his own vomit after a drunken binge and no one called an ambulance or a doctor as he lay gagging at a party in Albert Park.

Ray Read was the evil genius of the practical joke. He would tell people he was my brother and that I was adopted from a children's home for the mentally retarded. He told a girlfriend of mine that I had been operated on so that I could not father children because insanity ran in my family.

He put small fish hooks in chunks of meat and then fed them to friends' dogs. He would inject caustic soda into cartons of milk in his friends' fridges. He would pour caustic soda into the fish tanks at people's homes. He would have people's cars towed away, would call them ambulances when they weren't sick and would call the cops with tip-offs that his mates were dealing in drugs or harbouring escaped convicts.

He was the master of spreading false rumours and stories that wives and girlfriends of mates had VD. He would light small fires when invited to weddings; he pinched a bloke's widow on the bum at the funeral. He would drop shotgun shells in fires at barbecues just before he left the party. His list of tricks were endless.

He once took an old, 79-year-old senile woman shopping in

Richmond and then dumped her. She was lost for 24 hours, wandering the streets. Oh yes, he was a laugh a minute, all right.

When Ray got married he stuck 50-cent pieces to mousetraps so they would sink and placed them in a soapy bubble bath for his new bride. The marriage lasted five weeks.

Now, I felt this was just too much. Ray had a hot tub in his backyard. It was full and he used it daily. Dave the Jew and I had a plan to electrify it to kill Ray.

In the end we just placed three very strong rabbit traps in the bottom. Ray spent three weeks in hospital. He lost four toes — hence the name 'Six Toes.'

I must say that I liked the bastard. He was funny, but he went too far.

THE best laid plans of mice and men go wrong in the underworld as often as in any other field of endeavour. Nothing can be planned 100 per cent beforehand and that relates tenfold when it comes to the clinical science of murder.

I remember that in 1977 I made four separate attempts on the life of one particular fellow. He trusted me and I was one of the few fellows he would let through the front door.

The first time I went around I was about to pull out my sawn-off 12-gauge shotgun and blow his brains out while his back was turned. Just at the wrong moment, the bloody doorbell rang. He answered it and there was a young girl collecting for the Lord Mayor's Appeal. She got a good long look at my face while he went to get some money, so I put it down to experience and went home.

My second attempt found his mother at home with him enjoying tea and cakes. I've never been one to break up a happy family, so again I held my fire.

My third attempt was foiled when there was a knock on the door about a minute after I arrived. It was a lady friend of his. The fourth time he just let me in and the phone rang. He answered it and said, 'Hello. Oh nothing, Chopper's just called round.' Little did he know that these words saved his life; my presence in the house had been blurted out to some unknown person at the other end of the line.

I didn't make any further attempts. The guy was a bloody jinx — either that or a greater power was protecting him. He would never have suspected that on four different occasions sheer dumb luck saved his life.

I will not mention his name as he ended up becoming a bloody good mate of mine and I never had the heart to tell him that I was a hair's breadth away from killing him.

There wasn't that much money in it any rate.

DEAD LUCKY

Me and Micky shot him, I put one in his head.
Zipped one through the brain that made him nice and dead.
Micky drove the car
Up the bush, not too far.
Stan was in the boot, with the lid down tight.
Then we saw the cop car and the flashing blue light.
It was his lucky night, lucky to leave alive.
All he wanted to do was check for .05.

CHAPTER 9

A HITCHHIKER'S GUIDE TO THE GALLOWS

'HOW ARE YOUNG OFFENDERS TO BE TAUGHT
CORRECT RESPECT FOR LAW AND ORDER
WITHOUT THE AID OF A SOUND FLOGGING?'

THE former British hangman, Albert Pierrepoint, who sent 450 people to their deaths via the rope and the trapdoor, was the true master. For him, hanging was a family tradition and he loved his work.

Albert's Uncle Tom was a hangman for more than 40 years, and his dad was also a dab hand at the art of stretching necks. But Albert Pierrepoint was the master. He was the hangman for 25 years and his speed and skill was equal to, if not swifter than, that of his old Uncle Tom.

With 433 men and 17 women to his credit, Albert was a true authority on the topic of the death penalty. After he gave up his work he wrote his autobiography in 1974, and it was a book I greatly enjoyed.

He said that all the condemned men and women that he faced at their final moment convinced him that what he had done had not prevented a single murder. He became a campaigner for the abolition of the death penalty.

But, while Albert believed that he didn't prevent a single murder, he should have remembered that he prevented those he hanged from doing it again. And that's why I believe in capital punishment in some cases. It may not scare others so they don't do it, but it stops those who have been convicted from doing it again. In the case of crimes against children and sex killings, I do believe in the ultimate penalty.

There has been talk of bringing back the rope for killing police or prison officers. What rubbish. In most cases they are armed and able to protect themselves. Why they should rate in the scale of crimes above killing a seven-year-old girl is beyond my powers of reasoning. The weak should be protected: the young, women and the elderly. These are the people who should be protected first. The people who hurt them should be punished the hardest.

In most cases rough and tough coppers and prison officers don't need help. Bring back the rope for those who prey on the weak.

FOR all those Left-wing do-gooders who want to 'love' criminals back to the right track, let me say that as one who knows, they are on the wrong tram. And for those who think that putting crims in jail for 20 years is going to change things — well, they're wrong as well.

I would like to see the re-introduction of the lash as a means of punishment. In most cases, serving time in jail is a stupid waste of time. Sometimes jail may be the only answer but, in other cases, the lash could be the alternative.

Crimes of lightweight violence, from common assault to grievous bodily harm could be punished with a dozen or so cuts with the lash. I could have handled that instead of a few minor prison sentences.

Some of the young crims around do jail time too easily, and some drug dealers are well looked after on the inside. I think that a few cuts with the lash could add some dash to some of the wimps about and make men of them.

Things are getting too soft and easy all around. We need to get some discipline and backbone back into Australia. We need to bring the strap and the cane back into the school system, and the lash back into the prison system.

A nice bit of sharp pain clears the mind and cleanses the soul. I personally see the lash as a bloody good character builder. If you can't hang them, lash them and if you can't lash them, bash them.

Speaking of which, there is not enough bashing going on in police stations in these modern and enlightened times. The limp-wristed approach seems to be the order of the day.

The old 'toss the bastard down the stairs' type of police questioning seems to be a dying art. Now it is 'can I get you a cup of tea, sir, and I am sorry to bother you when you must be busy' approach. The old telephone book over the back of the head 50 or 100 times, the baton over the kneecaps, the loaded gun in the mouth and a good kicking seems to be almost a thing of the past.

I can remember the old lines: 'He attacked us, your Honour, so 12 of us were forced to restrain him.' I mean, where has it all gone? Police questioning is no longer the fun it used to be. How are young offenders to be taught correct respect for law and order without the aid of a sound flogging?

Police questioning has become, to be frank, quite boring. The bleeding hearts have won the day. Greenies in the bush, and Lefties in the city. What the hell has happened to us?

The tough approach at least produced tougher crooks, not like today. When police questioned via the use of fist, boot and baton, it produced a tough, hard breed of stand-up criminal.

I believe the soft approach towards the criminal of today is creating a weak, cowardly, limp-wristed, evil-minded, treacherous sort of snake-like crim. They behave more like spoilt, wilful children than hard crims.

The criminal of today, is, in my opinion, powder puff scum. Whereas a tough crim will not pick on the weak, the scum prey only on the weak.

NO LAST NAMES

Where did Tony go to?
Gone to the land of Oz,
I asked Dicky why,
And Dicky said because,
Tony talked out of school,
He broke the crooks' golden rule.
Dicky didn't need a hand,
Now Tony lives in magic land.
So who is Tony, who is Dick?
No last names, so there's the trick.

CHAPTER 10

SWORD SWALLOWERS AND DOUBLE AGENTS

'SHE HAD POLICEMEN PAYING HER RENT —
AND CRIMS BUYING HER CLOTHES.'

ONE of the prettiest girls I have ever seen was Pauline, a glamorous dancer who drove men to distraction.

She was a stripper who could send men crazy with her moves, but she got into heroin in a big way. She turned into a faded beauty working in Fitzroy Street, St Kilda, as a $60 whore.

Whenever I saw Pauline she was sporting a busted lip, black eye or a bruised face. She was constantly being bashed, raped and robbed for her hard-earned money or the drugs she needed.

I felt sorry for her, and regularly stopped to speak to her. She used to like the people of Fitzroy Street to see me chatting with her. She used to use my name to protect her. It did help her out, but not with some of her clients.

I once saw her walking towards me, 'smacked' off her face, in a torn-up T-shirt, a pair of tiny shorts that nearly cut her in half and a pair of spiky high heels.

She still had a body on her and a dancer's walk, more a strut than a walk. Her face was swollen and black and she had black, red and blue welts from her ankles to her bum and all over her body. You could see all this as she was wearing so little.

She had been thrashed with a man's leather belt by two men who had picked her up. This pair of vermin had taken her to a motel room, given her a hit of heroin, then doubled up on her and belted her for nearly an hour, just for fun. At the end, they took the money out of her purse. They had also smashed her false teeth and busted her ear drum. There she was, toothless, half dead, with a broken nose and beaten black and blue.

What could I, or anyone, do for her? Her arms were like dart boards, with needle marks scarring them up and down. She would offer me free sex and I would politely refuse. I didn't want to screw her, or bash her or rape her. And she just wanted someone to talk to.

She thought I was her friend. I wasn't. She was just a pathetic street animal and I felt sorry for her, the way you feel sorry for a lost dog.

She would talk about the old days and the past when she was a beautiful dancer. She would talk about the friends she used to have and how she was going to get on a methadone programme and pull her life into gear.

She would say that if she had a guy like me to look after her she would be as right as rain. She would talk about her clients and how the police would arrest her and toss her in the cells with the drunks.

I would not have touched her without the protection of rubber gloves, a stainless steel condom and a bucket of Dettol. But after a chat with me she would walk away, swinging her hips, then she would take the stance with her long legs apart on the street. Within no time at all, a car would pull up and the driver would invite her in.

The last time I saw her she had stepped on a nail and the wound looked septic to me. She walked with a limp in her high heels. She was still without her teeth and was full of VD and had not been able to get to the clinic. She had sores on her arms from the needles. Even then, she still had the legs of a dancer, but she had the face of the street gutter junkie.

She was so well-known as a health risk in St Kilda she had to find a new patch and was working in Footscray. She had ulcers inside her mouth and was catering for the perverted sex trade for $25 a go. She was sleeping in Salvation Army clothing bins.

She was a walking public toilet. Heroin was her only reason for living.

Pauline was the saddest human sight I had ever seen. But what of the human scum who used her, the sexual sickies? What a wonderful world we live in.

Pauline was a terrible example of the living dead, a heroin whore, a pathetic waste of life. Is she still alive?

It would be a mercy if she wasn't.

RANDY Mandy was a tall (5'9") blonde with a body that was put together by the devil in a wet dream. She was all legs and boobs. When she filled out official forms she gave her occupation as 'sword swallower'. I like a girl with a sense of humour.

She was never involved in prostitution, but she did work part time as a stripper and erotic dancer.

She was also a dab hand as a double agent, doing big favours and passing info from one side to the other. She slept with both the cops and the crooks.

Her main boyfriend was a big, bent Victorian detective I will call ... but then again, perhaps I won't. But she had plenty of others — and a lot more who wanted to get in the queue. She had boyfriends in both the Federal and Victorian forces, and a host of admirers in the criminal world.

Mandy was never trusted, but she was far too good-looking to kill or arrest. She had policemen paying her rent — and crims buying her clothes. She had top of the range jewellery, and if she ever wanted drugs, for recreational use, she would be provided with them.

She could get what she wanted from either side. She would put on strip shows at police stag nights or turn up to orgies at some top crims' homes.

She is about six years older than me and looks about ten years younger. She is terrified of violence, but fascinated and drawn to violent men.

When she was 38 she had an 18-year-old boyfriend, more a lackey than a companion. He was the errand boy, the house maid. I once called in to visit her. She greeted me at the door wearing nothing but a pair of stiletto high heels and a smile that took my breath away. I walked into the room, armed to the teeth, to warn her there was a police car outside. She put her fingers to her lips and said, 'Shh, he's asleep,' as the policeman slept like a baby in the next room. She was an energetic girl.

She was a crime groupie, fascinated with the criminal and the police world. Women with her unique physical and mental makeup are as rare as diamonds — and cause just as much trouble. But Mandy herself floated unharmed like a butterfly in a world where many other women have died.

Mad Charlie, the man who in the 1970s stood over the massage industry, was quite smitten with Mandy. He was like a little kid in her company, being ever so polite and correct. It was almost like a courtship and quite funny to see. The monster of a 1,000 massage parlours hopelessly in love with a lady, who in her high heels, looked down on Charlie as if he was a schoolboy.

He spent a small fortune on assorted presents, but the competition was too hot. She had more engagement rings than the local pawn shop. When he found out the truth of her police contacts, his heart hardened. Many people believe that Mad Charlie was shot over a woman.

Charlie's luck in love was always bad. His bodyguard, 'Big Mick', was also in love with Mandy, so it was a no-win situation.

For Mandy there is a happy ending. She is now living in a state of relaxed retirement in a Melbourne suburb with a young boyfriend. She no longer sees men from either world. However, I am told that should a face from the past drop in, she has far too kind a heart to turn away a man in distress.

This lady has caused men to be bashed, stabbed, shot, sent to prison and murdered. Yet, through it all, she has been untouchable, proving that physical and sexual charm can cripple the mind, heart and common sense of any man, be he copper or crook.

I know men who have gone to see Mandy with every intention of killing her, only to end up totally in love and lust. She was a unique classic, a freak.

The only person who nearly turned Mandy into a born-again virgin and a candidate for the nunnery was that old mad drug dealer, Scottish Steve.

Steve had arranged to sell Mandy to some Arabic seamen from a merchant ship bound for North Africa. They were prepared to pay $5,000 as they could re-sell her when they got to Africa.

It was a close call for Mandy, as Scottish Steve was convinced that she was some form of witch with evil powers and was trying to put a spell on him. Now, Scottish Steve was as mad as a bathtub full of rattlesnakes. She went to see him in tears. I do not know what took place in Scottish Steve's Ascot Vale home, but when she emerged, all was forgiven.

Steve announced that Mandy had been cleansed of all sin and that she was really a good girl at heart.

The mind boggles as to how she talked her way out of that one. Oh well, we all use the weapons that God gave us. Ha, ha.

WHILE Mandy was the top of the range in the crime groupie stakes, a sex legend, there was another girl who, on the strength of her outrageous behaviour, was known far and wide in the 1970s.

She was a big girl, with long black hair and gypsy looks, which might be why they called her Midnight. She could fight like a man and was more violent than most.

Midnight was totally without shame and would put on some of the wildest displays ever seen in Melbourne. She was a famous dirty girl, who mixed with some of the top crims of the 1970s.

She was rock solid in a police station and apart from having an insane sexual reputation, she was considered a solid chick.

The last time I saw her, she was on the way to the doctor with a billiard ball stuck in her bottom, and it was so uncomfortable she couldn't even read the news. But she was laughing her head off over her predicament, telling me I'd missed a great party.

Midnight was a wild lady, and I use the term lady purely because I am such a polite chap. She was the gangbang queen of Melbourne in the 1970s.

She was without shame and could make a gunman blush with her behaviour. And often did.

I HAVE mentioned before that over the years I have received some tragic letters from old grannies and tearful mothers whose sons and daughters have died of drug overdoses.

I understand and sympathise with them, but I also get some weird and wonderful letters from some people who should have been locked up long before me. The assortment of Jesus freaks, bible bashers, violence junkies, murder nuts and other fruitcakes that have contacted me by mail indicates we are not a well country.

Most of this mail has gone in the bin. But the first book has produced a steady flow of mail different to anything I have had before. It is clear to me now that every nut in Australia must end up inside bookshops, because just about every one of them has written to me. They have all come out of hiding, and I wish most of them would crawl back under their rocks.

Most of the letters are full of crap but occasionally you get one from someone worthwhile. One person who has been writing to me for some years is a delightful lady, Jackie. She has become a loyal 'penfriend', if you can believe it. She tells me she is the President of the Chopper Read fan club. She even has a T-shirt confirming the fact.

Well, while I enjoy the joke I would like to tell her not to wear that particular item of clothing in certain less reputable areas of Melbourne because some people might rip it straight off her chest. Perhaps not such a bad idea.

Another girl with obvious literary taste is Karen. She wrote to me to tell me that the cover of the first book would make an excellent tattoo. I took that with a grain of salt. A tongue-in-cheek fan club with a T-shirt is one thing but a tattoo, like herpes, is forever.

Karen is known as the 'White Dove'. She said I was bigger than Batman. I just hope she never meets my mate 'The Penguin'.

I had mixed feelings about the tattoo business. To be truthful, I didn't believe it was true.

When Jackie sent me the photo of herself with the T-shirt I thought, This is a chick with a different sense of humour. But when I saw the pictures of Karen with the book cover illustration tattooed on her back, I realised she was very serious indeed. Obviously, she loved the book.

Receiving mail in prison can be one of the great delights. It really helps break the loneliness. But it can be depressing, too. I get letters from battered wives and frightened women who ask me for advice. Some of the letters are quite sad, and I try to reply with the best advice I can, feeling a little like Dear Abby. Chopper the agony aunt.

One lovely young lady who has written to me is Desiree. She knows that I haven't any children myself so I am sort of a godfather to her daughter, Gemma. She is a lovely little girl who also writes to me. So when I say the book brought some whackos out of the woodwork, I must admit that not all the letters come from mental patients. But there is no doubt that I am a pin-up boy for the nuts of the world. And do I ever get some mail from them, bless their pointy little heads.

But if someone writes to me in their own blood after cutting off their ears, that's when I'll change my name and get plastic surgery.

I have even received mail from blokes who have told me they read the book and thought I looked nice ... so could I send them a photo. Bloody Hell. Needless to say, I did not reply. The next thing they will want me to be the May Queen at the Gay Mardi Gras.

When I get letters from people asking me in a roundabout way how to fix their domestic upsets, I scratch my head. Now Chopper Read can be many things to many people, but one thing I will never be is a marriage guidance counsellor. Some people write to ask how much it would cost to fix a problem and I certainly don't agree with giving quotes on a bit of paper.

Some people have written to me claiming to be related, others have said they were related to me in a former life. One claimed that I appeared in a dream and passed on a special message. I sincerely hope it was 'get some help, you crazy creep'.

One woman, who signed her name 'Zandra', said she was a mystic witch, a mistress of the black arts. She claims that my real name is not Mark Brandon Read but 'Zeath' and that I was her warlock brother and that if we both prayed at the same time we could double our mystic powers.

I flushed Zandra's letter down the toilet. Let's see her spook her way out of that.

One of the great problems of being in jail is that every nutcase out there knows your address. Let me out.

IN the world of prostitution, standover tactics are part of life. Girls get bashed, robbed and raped. Few complain, as they long ago lost their dignity and pride. Without self-respect, they are victims waiting to happen.

But not all ladies of loose morals are easy victims.

There was one prostitute who managed a small parlour in Prahran who stood about six feet tall and could have taken up a career on the catwalk had she been so inclined in her younger days. Her name was Lucy.

In those days Lucy had two girls working for her who were in their late teens. One night they had a visit from a group of AFL footballers from a well-known club.

The footballers were loud and drunk, celebrating a football victory. They got a little violent and refused to pay the service fee.

They locked the door and raped all three women. Then they left without paying.

About a week later they came back, with a few more in the pack, for a repeat performance, only to find 'Juicy Lucy' standing in the doorway with a double-barrelled shotgun. She screamed, 'You bastards aren't going to get away with this again.'

She bashed a big ruckman in the head with the butt of the gun, cutting him badly, then fired one barrel over the head of the rest of them. There were footballers everywhere running for their lives.

They might be heroes to mugs, old women and little kids, but AFL footballers don't count for much in the underworld. And as any working girl can tell you, they have a poor reputation in the parlours as loud-mouthed drunks who complain about the entrance fee.

LADY KILLER

I never killed a lady, and I really don't know why,
Most of the ones I've met have really deserved to die,
I guess in the end,
In spite of my mind being bent,
I'm just a bloody old softy,
A real old-fashioned gent.

CHAPTER 11

TEH CURSE OF THE BOOKIE ROBBERY (OR WHY I NEVER EAT DIM SIMS)

' "CHOPPER," HE SAID, "I COULD BUTCHER THE AUSTRALIAN CRIMINAL WORLD IF I HAD A DOZEN LIKE YOU." '

IT *was perhaps the most precise, well-planned armed robbery ever committed in Australia.*

The plan was hatched in a cell of an English prison. The gang was hand-picked and taken to a remote area in country Victoria to train and to get the timing down to seconds. The leader knew that to avoid a shoot-out, everything would have to work perfectly.

It culminated in a breathtaking raid on the Victorian Club in Queen Street on April 26, 1976. The gang escaped with somewhere between $1.4 and $12 million. The true total was never really known as the bookies were coy about how much was in their bags that day.

The leader of the gang was Raymond Patrick Chuck Bennett, a career criminal with a taste for the high life. He was tough and a born leader.

Several months before, Bennett had slipped into Australia while on a week's pre-release leave from Parkhurst Prison. He was seen at the time by a young policeman at Moonee Ponds. Bennett flew back to England satisfied that the job could be done. When he finished his sentence he returned to set up the audacious robbery.

Bennett's robber recruits each had specific roles to practise at their secret training camp. Like a football coach, Bennett told them to give up women and drinking during the training. But, like footballers, many of them slipped out to disobey the coach's orders. They spent months training. Each was confident he knew what to do.

One man, who was in charge of the stolen cars, later went on to become an international criminal. He was eventually convicted over drug matters and was sentenced to a long prison term.

A time-and-motion expert recruited for the job was little known to police. He was later found to have helped organise several of the country's biggest stick-ups. He eventually was sentenced over an armed robbery in Sydney.

The gang of about nine decided to hit the bookies on April 26 because they knew the amount of cash on settling would be huge. The bookies had to settle for three meetings over the Easter break.

According to former Deputy Commissioner Paul Delianis, the Great Bookie Robbery crew was probably the most polished armed robbery gang in Australia. 'They specialised in commando-like raids for years,' he said. 'They copied the style of an English group of criminals called the Wembley Gang, which used similar tactics.'

No one was ever convicted over the bookie robbery and most of the money was laundered overseas. When Bennett's aged mother collapsed in a solicitor's office one day ambulance officers who cut her clothing away to give her cardiac massage found $90,000 hidden underneath.

But justice sometimes moves in mysterious ways. After the bookie robbers became the talk of the criminal world many of those allegedly involved in the robbery did not live to spend the money.

Bennett himself was gunned down in the Melbourne Magistrates' Court on November 12, 1979, by a brazen killer, probably Brian Kane. It was believed to be a payback for the murder of Leslie Herbert Kane, who had gone missing from his Wantirna home in 1978. Brian Kane was later shot dead in a Brunswick hotel.

Ian Revell Carroll went on to become one of the best organisers of armed robberies in Australia. He was killed in a gun battle in the backyard of his rented Mt Martha home in 1983.

Anthony Paul McNamara continued to associate with criminals. He was found dead of a heroin overdose, allegedly from a drug hotshot, in Easey Street, Collingwood in 1990.

Another member fled to outback Western Australia after he was marked for death.

Two brothers involved graduated to organising their own stick-ups. One is now in jail serving a long sentence.

Norman Leung Lee was the man who was allegedly given the task of laundering the cash from the job. It was alleged some of the money was used to buy equipment for his dim sim factory. The rest was allegedly invested in land and international drug and arms deals.

Lee was shot dead by police, allegedly as he tried to rob an armed van at Melbourne Airport in July 1992.

Lee, 44, had been charged 16 years earlier with laundering $124,000 in cash from the bookie robbery. He refused to talk to police and stood silently while they cut open his safe looking for money from the robbery. It was empty, and he was acquitted.

It was an era of gunmen who planned big armed robberies. It was a time just before drugs took over the underworld. And it was a time when gangs of vicious criminals preyed on their own: headhunters or toecutters would torture armed robbers to get a piece of the action.

IN the 1970s there were some real hard men about, old-style crims. Thinkers with dash, men who had the brains to devise a plan and the guts to carry it out. In that era there were none better than Ray Chuck Bennett. He was one of the real tough guys I have known. I was proud to call 'Chuckles' my friend because he was a bloody good bloke. The human scum who cheered and celebrated at the news of his death are not forgotten and, like all cowards, will get theirs in the end.

Ray Chuck, which I think was his original name before he took the name 'Bennett', was a thinker and a top gang war tactician. He was also a master planner and one of the Australian underworld's foremost bank robbers. Without Ray Chuck's thinking the Great Bookie Robbery would never have been pulled off.

Ray was a criminal leader whose personal courage gave strength to the men who followed him. Russell 'Mad Dog' Cox, widely considered to be Australia's greatest bank robber and a man whose thinking ability, physical courage and mental coolness is a legend in the criminal world, was a true and loyal friend of Ray Chuck's. However, in Ray's company Cox was a follower, never a leader, which gives an insight into the leadership abilities of the man.

The war between Ray and his crew and the Kane brothers is now part of Australian criminal folklore. They were the two top Melbourne crews and they destroyed each other in a sea of blood all over Brian Kane's massive ego and powerful waterfront and criminal following, not to mention Ray's personal pride. He refused to take a backward step or give an inch. A little-known fact was that as a younger man Ray acted as bodyguard for waterfront strongman Billy 'the Texan' Longley. Long after Ray Chuck left Longley's company the enemies he made in those early days with Billy remained with him.

The truth about the war between Ray Chuck and Brian Kane is simple. They didn't like each other as kids and grew up hating each other more and more. In the name of peace and common sense they would from time to time over the years give each other a hello across a public bar. Kane would offer a loud greeting with Chuck returning a curt and firm nod of that hard head of his.

Deep down, Chuck believed the Kane brothers to be police informers under the personal care of a well-known Melbourne policeman. Ray Chuck was a thousand per cent criminal and he described Brian Kane as 'half a policeman'.

What happened had to happen. It could end no other way. As for the Kanes trying to stand over Ray and his crew over the proceeds of the bookie robbery — thus supposedly starting the final blood war that destroyed both sides — the real reason for the final conflict was never so grand. In fact, it began over a bloody fist fight in the Royal Oak Hotel in Richmond that started with an exchange of insults between Kane and Chuck and resulted in Brian Kane being beaten in front of his friends and hangers-on.

Threats of death towards the wife and children of Chuck made by a drunken Les Kane simply brought to the boil a hatred that had been simmering for 20 years. The line was drawn and sides were taken. Chuck attacked, and like the general he was he broke the Kane empire apart and drowned them in their own blood.

Les Kane simply went on the missing list.

The story is that a frightened, panic-stricken Brian Kane, while in hiding, reached out for his old protector — a very tough policeman — and the late Christopher Dale 'Rentakill' Flannery, and they plotted, set up and carried out the death of Ray Chuck in the Melbourne magistrate's court. It was a classic and unbelievable underworld killing that is today part of Australian criminal folklore.

Some people might find it hard to believe the rumour that one of 'Victoria's finest' could be involved in such a crime. And I, of course, would dismiss such suggestions as foul slander and gossip. As far as the policeman was concerned, it was one of the hairiest yarns I have ever heard.

The murder, not long after, of Brian Kane (in the Quarry Hotel in Brunswick) was simply a 'mopping up' action carried out far too late by a broken-hearted and blood-loyal friend of Ray Chuck's. With Chuck dead, there was no joy or celebration at the news of Brian Kane's death. Chuckles was gone, and a thousand Kanes in their graves couldn't bring him back. I cheered at the news of Les Kane's death, but I didn't cheer at Brian's. Ray was dead and it was all too late.

After I was betrayed and stabbed seven times in H Division in 1979, Ray Chuck, who was in H Division at that time, came in to my labour yard to see me. He showed me great kindness. He cheered me up and encouraged me to get well and get back into it bigger and badder than ever.

'Chopper,' he said, 'it's one big, bloody kennel, and most of the good blokes are double agents and dogs and secret policemen. And the rest of the pricks are too weak to even talk about. You make your own rules, you run your own race, you fight your own fights and live your own life ... and if anybody doesn't like it and wants to rock'n'roll, bury the maggots. It's not a popularity contest, Chopper.'

THERE is a story about Ray Chuck that I cannot vouch for as the truth, but he told it to me and Jimmy Loughnan when he was in B Division of Pentridge for a short time in 1975, and it's worth telling.

Ray's version of the story is that when he was in prison in England he found himself in the same jail as Reggie Kray, one half of the dreaded Kray twins, my boyhood heroes who ruled the London underworld and nightclub scene for more than a decade. According to Ray he got into an argument with Kray and blows were thrown and Ray won the fight, sending Kray to the floor bleeding and beaten.

Great story, but I didn't want to believe it. I'm not saying that Ray Chuck couldn't have held his own in a fight with Kray, but he could never have beaten him in an English prison and survived. However, the story was believed by all who heard the yarn ... until the toecutter they called 'The Pom' heard it. He roared laughing, as he had heard a different version of events from friends of his in England, ex-members of the Kray firm like himself.

According to 'The Pom' there had been some sort of fight — with Reg Kray winning — and with Ray Chuck yelling verbal threats. Ray was later grabbed and beaten in the showers by a crew of East End crooks who were on Reggie Kray's team in jail. Ray continued to show disrespect for Reg Kray and although no more violence took place there was ill-will. When Ray got out he was kidnapped at the gate by a car-load of East End boys and given a bloody good flogging and driven to Heathrow Airport and told he'd taken a right liberty by mouthing off at Reg Kray. He was told if he returned to London he would go home in a box.

My opinion is that if the story is even half true, I can't understand how Ray ever got out alive. The Kray twins invented the torture business. As I've said, I think the world of Ray Chuck, but it gave me the shits to hear him say he'd punched on with Reg Kray and won. The other version is much more acceptable, to my way of thinking.

ONE Kane I did like and respect was old Reg Kane, father of Brian, Les and Ray. I first met him in a hotel in Port Melbourne in 1972 in the company of Horatio Morris. In fact, it was old Reg who pulled me to one side and advised me to watch old Horatio, who was a stone-killing hard man, and friendship would have meant nothing to him if I put a hole in my manners even by accident.

Horatio would shoot you in the head just as a lesson 'not to do it again'. Old Reg was genuinely concerned about my future wellbeing while mixing in the company of Horatio Morris. Reg was a great old fellow, a gentleman with a kind, generous, caring heart who felt sorry for people. He was always a soft touch for a good sob story and a much-loved and respected man: even the blood enemies of his three sons held no ill-will towards him. He was a hard man of the old school whereas his three sons, for all their swagger and bully-boy violence and fearful reputation, were never in their father's class.

Reg grew up smacking the bottoms of men like his sons, and as much as he loved them, he was never overly impressed when stories of his sons' conduct and talk of their fearful reputation and their so-called fighting ability reached his ears. Reg was a real hard man, while his boys dreamt of being hard men and pretended and played the role. I often suspected that Reg was at times embarrassed when Brian and Les swaggered into the pub bunging on their tough-guy routine.

WHILE I was never friends with Brian Kane and we stood in two separate camps, we were never bitter enemies and didn't hate each other. We simply did not trust one another. I personally felt that his reputation within the Melbourne criminal world was vastly overrated.

However, I will give credit where credit is due. Brian was a violent, cunning criminal who had the bulk of the criminal world and the waterfront bluffed, beaten and baffled. Why he got away with it for so long was a puzzle to me. However, Brian and his semi-retard brother Les did get away with it for well over a decade, so my hat goes off to them.

A small touch of comedy I will mention about Brian. He always was concerned that he might be charged with carrying a gun, but he also knew it would be unsafe for him to walk down to the milk bar unarmed. He came up with this brilliant plan that he would hide his shooter in the handbag of any girl he was with at the time.

I told him once that when the day came that he did get blown away he would be found with his hand stuck in a bloody handbag, which was no way for a hard crim to go out. My attitude was that if you don't carry your gun on you, you might as well not have a gun at all.

Anyway, my few words in jest proved true. When Brian did get blown away, with his last dying breath he was trying to get his bloody gun out of a handbag next to him. With his luck he probably would have grabbed the lipstick, and not even his colour, at that.

I cannot name the man who killed Brian Kane. However, it is no great secret in criminal circles who pulled the trigger. And he, too, felt that the old gun in the handbag trick was the height of good humour. For a rat-cunning, shifty, streetwise old hood Brian Kane certainly died dumb.

ANOTHER person from that era was old Normie Lee, Dim Sim Normie, Chinese Normie, call him what you like. He was one of the quiet men of the Melbourne criminal world. He was involved with Ray Chuck's crew, mostly in the thinking department.

Normie didn't run around mouthing off or trying to shoot people in pubs. He was a loyal and trusted behind-the-scenes helper. It was always believed that Normie used money from the Great Bookie Robbery for Chuckles and the crew. There have been a number of rumours that several people went on the missing list via Normie's Dim Sim machines and came out in tasty tid bits for public consumption, Les Kane among them. However, that was only rumour, although I have tended to steer clear of dimmies since then. Call me delicate, if you like.

I found Normie to be gentle, polite and good-natured, but very secretive and a touch paranoid. For Normie to die such a violent death was out of character. I know many men who I think could end up dying in a gun battle and Normie just wasn't one of them. He was just another member of Ray's crew who lost his way after the death of the General.

THE king of the headhunters in this country was the man known far and wide in the underworld as 'Jimmy The Pom'. I won't use his real name because it would not be etiquette. Despite the mayhem and bloodshed behind him, Jimmy has never copped many serious convictions and he's retired now, so he might be a little offended if his real name was connected with the kidnapping, torture and murder his crew carried out here and in England over the years.

'The Pom' was the master of violence. He was a former mercenary, former member of the Kray brothers firm in London's East End and the IRA. His reputation for violence was not only Australia-wide but international.

'The Pom' was not strictly an accurate nickname for Jimmy, because his sympathies were with the Irish. He reputedly acted as personal bodyguard to the IRA deputy Joe Cahill in the early 1960s. Later, the story goes, he served under the famous mercenary 'Mad Mike Hoare' with his fifth commando unit in the Congo in 1964. He came to Australia in the late 1960s, and with a small crew of ex-IRA men and Sydney and Melbourne criminals, he started what became known and feared as the 'Toecutter Gang'.

This might be hard to understand, but to me 'The Pom' was a wonderful fellow. I'm nothing if not egotistical, and he flattered me — paying me the highest of compliments when I was only 24.

'Chopper,' he said, 'I could butcher the Australian criminal world if I had a dozen like you.'

'The Pom' backed Billy Longley in the bloody painters and dockers war in the 1970s. He was arrested in NSW for the murder of Jake

Maloney in 1972, was later acquitted on appeal, came to Victoria on weapons charges and then deported. The last I heard of him he was involved in business with Charlie Kray, the older brother of Reggie and Ronnie Kray. The word is that he is now retired in comfort, spending his summers in Spain with the rest of London's retired gangsters.

Jimmy was a friend and a teacher to me. I will never forget some of his sayings. One was: 'There is no mafia in Belfast' ... meaning that when it comes down to tin tacks, blood will beat money every time. Another saying of his was: 'Don't toss the party until the body's been buried.'

THERE are many stories about people like 'The Pom'. But the most fearsome is about the 'tattoo torture' job in NSW in the very early 1970s.

It happened when the toecutter gang kidnapped a payroll bandit and put him under heavy questioning as to where he had hidden $75,000. After removing every toe on his left foot and getting nowhere, they knew they had a tough bastard on their hands.

They laid the bandit on his front and held him firmly while they cut around the edges of the poor fellow's back — right around a big tattoo of an eagle fighting a dragon. Then they took a pair of pliers and slowly peeled the skin and tattoo off the fellow's back. They told me later it was like ripping leather. It took a fair amount of strength and care to remove the full back job tattoo. The blood-curdling screams stopped half-way through the operation. It was thought by all concerned that the fellow had simply passed out. However, when they tried to revive him, it was found that the poor bugger had died.

They thought about this. They figured no man would suffer the tortures of hell simply to protect money. No man could endure the insane pain of being skinned alive after having his toes cut off just to safeguard the whereabouts of a few rolls of paper. Then they realised that although the bandit wouldn't lay down his life for money alone, he might do it for love. The guy had died for love, not money.

The answer was that the money must be in the possession of the payroll bandit's wife, and he had died to protect her. The toecutters wrapped the tattoo skin in plastic and a member of his gang visited the wife, a beautiful woman who had been a loyal and loving wife to the bandit for 20 years since they had been teenage sweethearts.

She asked, 'Is he alive?'

The answer was 'Yes ... give us the money and you can have him.'

She paid the money over. Then they told her that the operation was a success ... but the patient had died.

Postscript: the woman in question never went to the police. I was told by a gang member a long time later that she was the strongest lady he'd ever met in his life. And the look on her face is still a memory that haunts him to this day.

I would describe it as one of his few regrets. Maybe his only one.

A TOECUTTER very close indeed to 'Jimmy The Pom' and a well-known dockie just as close to Billy 'The Texan' Longley were rumoured to be responsible for the death of Alfred 'The Ferret' Nelson, a painter and docker who went on the missing list in the early 1970s during the dockies' wars.

Nelson's car was pulled out of the water near South Wharf. It is believed by some who should know that 'The Ferret' died a very painful death indeed, and that the toecutter mentioned above was in charge of proceedings. The story goes that before they filled in the grave the painter and docker urinated on Nelson's mortal remains.

The toecutter was a blood and guts boy from way back, but he could not abide what he called 'bad manners'. He pulled out a .45

automatic and told the dockie, 'If you don't put your dick away in two seconds I'll blow the bloody thing off.'

The dockie, one of the toughest men on the Australian waterfront, obeyed with such haste that he wet his pants. Or so the story goes.

Of course, I could never admit that a man close to 'The Pom' told me this story first hand or in the first person, and I'll have to put it down as just another old criminal yarn.

'The Pom' played by hard rules, yet he also had a strange sense of fair play and correct conduct. When he was with Mad Mike Hoare in the fifth commando unit in the Congo in the mid-1960s he was asked to question a suspected informer. There is a scurrilous allegation that he removed the man's eyes with a teaspoon before questioning — yet refused to allow torture below the belt, as he could not abide crude conduct. Strange man.

There is a story that Jimmy walked into a Sydney hotel and an acquaintance remarked to him that it was a 'nice day'. Without a word Jimmy pulled out his gun and smashed the fellow across the face and said, 'When I want a weather report I'll ask for one.' What a comic.

THINKING about 'The Pom' and his adventures brings back the name of a well-known underworld figure, Johnny Regan, the so-called 'vice king of Sydney'. Regan was a hoon — a common or garden pimp — a criminal pastime that in NSW is seen as a good job if you can get it. In Melbourne, a hoon or pimp is one step up the social ladder from a rockspider. Men involved in living off the earnings of women are regarded by right-thinking people as scum, bludgers, pimps and arsewipes.

I will never forget the time when Regan was down for the Melbourne Cup once I showed him just what I thought of his reputation as a violent and highly dangerous man. We both ended up at the same party and his big talk and loud mouth drowned out all the others until I headbutted the fool to the ground.

I put the rat down three times before the old gunman Horatio Morris said to him, 'You'd better stay down, son, or he'll kill you.' And that was the last we heard of Johnny Regan until he got himself killed the following year. He was a joke, typical Sydney 'piss and wind'. He had plenty of razzle dazzle and 'We play rugby, aren't we tough' talk. I've never met a pimp who could fight, and Johnny Regan was a classic example. No doubt if I'd been a woman in a brothel he would have beaten me near to death.

If you're wondering what this has to do with 'Jimmy The Pom', stay tuned. To cut a long story short, rumour has it that he was the last person to see Regan alive. Naturally, I couldn't possibly vouch for the accuracy of this allegation, and I would put it down to foul slander and gossip. But in the interest of telling a good story I will recount this and other rumours just as I heard them from someone very close and dear to Jimmy himself.

'The Pom' was arrested for the murder of another toecutter called Jake Maloney, who had himself earlier killed Kevin Gore. 'The Pom' was rightly acquitted of the charge, but the rumour persisted that Maloney died because he wrongly advised that a body tossed into Sydney Harbour would be eaten by sharks. 'The Pom' knew nothing of sharks.

As it happened, a chap by the name of Baldy Blair was thrown in the harbour (he was dead at the time) and the rumour is that a certain toecutter was horrified to read in the newspapers that Baldy's body was not eaten by sharks at all, but washed up on the beach in Botany Bay.

The rumour is that the last words Maloney heard were: 'Sharks, hey, Jake. I'll give you bloody sharks, you idiot.' And then a gun went 'bang, bang' and that was the end of Jake. Of course, I do not believe for a moment that this reflects on the character of 'Jimmy The Pom', as it is nothing but gossip.

Mind you, if I had been an innocent bystander, and a policeman had asked me if I could describe the person who spoke those last words to Jake Maloney, I would point just below my chin and say, 'Only up to here.'

That's the sort of effect the old toecutter has on people's memories.

THE FUNERAL DIRECTOR

Have you ever seen a body on a cold dark night?
And even though he's dead, he can still give a fright,
Ever tried to dig a hole with garden spade?
Then shorten him at the kneecaps with the slice of the blade,
It's not an easy job, please take my word,
So forget the other stories you may have heard,
Dropping him in the hole, and trying to take care,
Then offering up to heaven a silent prayer,
And feeling a bit like God's garbage collector,
The underworld's answer to the funeral director.

CHAPTER 12

BOBBY BARRON AND THE BAD FAIRIES

'FOR ALL THE POLICE KNEW, BOBBY WAS
ATTACKED BY THE PHANTOM OF THE OPERA.'

IN the summer of 1974, Victorians were shaken out of their holiday mood by the news that a married Salvation Army couple had been senselessly murdered on a lonely road near Berwick.

The couple, Colonel Ronald Walter Smith, 65, and Minna Radcliffe Smith, 67, were on their way to take a gift of plums to relatives on January 17 when they were killed.

Colonel Smith had been shot in the head and chest, and his wife in the head, chest and shoulder.

Police believed the killer ordered the couple from their small 1968 white Mazda sedan, then executed them. He then tried to steal the car, but bogged it in soft ground caused by heavy summer rains. He was forced to abandon the car and flee. The dead man's body was found under the right rear wheel of the car, the woman's about two metres away. Police believe she was shot as she tried to run away after her husband was killed. Robert James Barron, then 25, was charged with the murders.

It was alleged Barron flagged the car down in Darling Road, East

Malvern, after a drinking session with a mate in a local hotel and ordered the couple to drive to a St Kilda flat, and later to Berwick.

A key Crown witness, Kevin Marsden, told the court that Barron later told him, 'I knocked them both. I must have been mad. I run them both over.'

Another witness told of finding the bodies. 'I saw the body of a male near the rear wheel of the car. His body had tyre marks on the body.'

After a six-day trial during which the defence did not offer evidence and Barron did not make a statement, he was found guilty.

At one stage he sacked his lawyer; he also yelled abuse at a witness. At the inquest he had to be removed from the court.

Before sentence Mr Justice Gillard said that he usually did not comment about a jury decision and only handed down the penalty.

'However, having regard to the evidence of this case, I must say I agree with the verdict of the jury. These were atrocious crimes with no redeeming feature, and it is very difficult to understand why anybody should have been guilty of such callousness and shocking conduct.'

It took the jury of seven women and five men just 75 minutes to reach the unanimous verdict of guilty.

As soon as the foreman declared the verdict, Barron cried out, 'You have just found an innocent man guilty. You're all murderers. How does it feel to be a murderer?'

One woman in tears at the back of the court yelled out, 'You bastards, what's he going to be like as an old man?'

Asked if he had anything to say before sentencing Barron said, 'There's no justice.' He then turned to a group of detectives who had given evidence against him and said, 'What about you, you bastards. You got Ryan hanged on hearsay, and now me.'

Barron was one of the last men in Victoria sentenced to death. The penalty was later commuted to life in prison. In 1976 he was sentenced to four months after he escaped from Pentridge Prison. He scaled the south wall of the jail but was recaptured within minutes.

The then head of the homicide squad, Mr Bill Walters, said he remembered Barron well. 'He was a violent criminal of his time who showed no remorse for what he had done. He was a person without compassion, or any redeeming features whatsoever.'

In 1992 he was still in custody and was considered insane.

THERE was a young chappie out at Pentridge Prison many years ago who was popular with most other crims, yet feared by them at the same time. As I was to find so often, I held a somewhat different view of the gentleman.

His name is Bobby Barron. He was the bloke who murdered two Salvation Army officers in the early 1970s when he wanted to steal their car — a bit much for a car, even for a bloke with my sensitive ways.

The Salvo husband and wife team gave him a lift when he was hitch-hiking and he repaid them by killing them in cold blood. Then he put their bodies under the back wheels of the car to try and get out of the bog.

Now I've always liked Salvos. I'd always buy a *Watchtower* when a Salvo came through the pub. Ask anyone, I've always been a bit of a softie. There was a wonderful fellow, a Salvo, who used to visit H Division to ask prisoners if they needed Christmas gifts to send to their children. This was the sort of Christian thing the Salvos would do, that the other religious types failed to bother with.

The Salvos would do things without any fuss or fanfare. I would watch with an eagle eye as a stream of so-called top gangsters and armed robbery men, some who would talk about the money they made in six-figure numbers, would tell their sob stories to the Salvo to get presents for their kids. It was pathetic to watch and see the big-talking gangsters take advantage of Christian charity. It was something I always remembered. They would rather spend their own money in jail on drugs and get the Salvos to provide the presents for the kids.

Barron was once a top streetfighter and an up and coming gunman, well connected with certain members of the underworld. But it is my expert opinion that the use of the drug LSD in the early 1970s sent him into a world of insanity from which he never returned.

I was with Bobby in B Division in 1975. He was then considered to be the fittest man in Pentridge. He was also as mad as a cut snake and had wild and crazy eyes. He refused to speak to anyone, which was fairly handy, because when he did he just didn't make sense. Other inmates were always a little on edge when he was around. He gave people the creeps. He was a spooky bastard.

Bobby and I met up again in H Division in 1976, after he escaped and was on the outside for all of about 20 seconds. Let me tell you, freedom did not help his equilibrium in the brain box department, if you get my meaning.

He walked around the Number Two Industry Yard of H Division with a razor blade in his pocket, and he was no apprentice barber, let me tell you. He would spend his days staring at me and Jimmy Loughnan. I was always taught that staring at someone was the height of bad manners, particularly if you carried a razor blade and carried on like an extra from *The Exorcist*.

So it was that Bobby Barron was carried out of the Number Two industry yard with his skull shattered in a dozen places with chips of skull bone, hair, skin and flesh splattered around the place.

Not a pretty sight. Particularly before dinner. From memory, it was steak-and-kidney pudding that night.

We all thought he would die, but he didn't. For some stupid reason the police interviewed Jimmy Loughnan and myself over poor Bobby's mishap. I told the police that I thought they were jumping to conclusions and had ignored the obvious — the attempted suicide angle of the case.

He may have been mad but Bobby Barron was a solid hard crim and he didn't give anyone up, and whoever did it was never brought to justice. No one in the Industry Yard saw anything ... Danny James was taking a piss, Johnny Price was washing his hands, Jimmy Loughnan was watching a bullant crawling up the wall and I was watching Jimmy Loughnan while he was watching the bullant. Sadly, none of us could help the police on this occasion, much as we would have liked.

For all the police knew, Bobby was attacked by the Phantom of the Opera. Allegations that Jimmy Loughnan pulled Bobby's coat while I caved his head in with a vice handle are, to repeat an often-used expression, foul gossip and slander.

The last I heard Bobby Barron was residing in J Ward at the Ararat Mental Hospital for the criminally insane. He may never again see the light of day. Years after the incident I met him in Jika Jika. I gave him a TV and a radio. He was like a small child in the mind.

Bobby thought he remembered what had happened in H Division. He told me he had been attacked by some bad fairies. He was totally gone ... maybe he should have run for Parliament.

ALEX THE ARAB

Alex the Arab was a hard old boy,
He had a plan, he had a ploy,
He fought Frankie first, and then he fought me,
Then out came the blade, and the Arab began to flee,
I went and got my mate Max,
A home-made, razor sharp, steel meat axe,
Alex didn't even know it was coming,
Twice in the brain, and I kept on running,
He didn't squeal, cry or squawk;
Bang in the head, with the old tomahawk.
Ha ha.

CHAPTER 13

RENTAKILL TAKES REDUNDANCY

'THE GUY WAS A MENTAL PEANUT WITH THE
PHYSICAL COURAGE OF DISHWATER.'

HE was feared in the NSW and Victorian underworld for more than a decade. A good-looking man with a cruel streak who would kill anyone if the price was right.

Christopher Dale Flannery, known to one and all as 'Rentakill', relished a reputation he earned after beating two separate murder charges.

Born in Brunswick in 1949, Flannery left school at 14. Ironically, his brother Ed chose the high road and ended up a successful barrister.

Chris, on the other hand, was a likeable young man until he was placed under pressure. Then he would respond with extreme violence. As a teenager he was sentenced to seven years for rape.

By the 1970s Flannery started to turn his naturally violent nature into profit. He taught himself the rudimentary elements of pathology — not to heat, but to hurt. He wanted to know exactly what bullets of different calibres would do when they entered the human body, and his interest wasn't academic.

Once, when Flannery was arrested at Geelong, he said he was sick and

*was taken to the toilet. He grabbed a small pistol from his underpants —
but was overpowered by police.*

*He was not a subtle man. As with most criminals, Flannery had his
fair share of tattoos; including one across his stomach, the word
'Lunchtime', with an arrow pointing to his groin.*

*For some time Flannery was close to the one-legged private
investigator, Tom Ericksen, a notorious figure in his own right.*

*In 1980 Flannery was charged with the murder of Melbourne
businessman, Roger Wilson.*

*In what was, to then, the longest murder trial in Victoria's history, it
was alleged that Flannery and another man were paid $35,000 to kill
Wilson. The Crown stated that the hitmen pretended to be detectives and
flagged down Wilson's green Porsche on the Princess Highway at
Cranbourne.*

*The unsuspecting businessman was handcuffed and taken to a lonely
spot to be killed. According to police the first shot failed to kill Wilson,
who then made a desperate break in the darkness.*

*He then ran blindly until he hit a paddock fence where Flannery fired
several shots into the body. Wilson's body has never been found.*

*The Crown alleged that Flannery drove Wilson's car to Tullamarine
where he left it in the long-term car park to give the impression that
Wilson had voluntarily staged his own disappearance.*

*Police were told that Flannery was berated by a woman for being
'sloppy' in the way he had killed Wilson.*

*A teenage girl, Debbie Boundy, was to have been a key witness in the
trial. She disappeared in 1981 from the car park of a Melbourne hotel. She
has not been seen since. It was alleged that she was lured from the pub
with the promise of some marijuana but was abducted and shot in the
head.*

Flannery was acquitted of the murder but his trouhles were far from over. As he walked from the Supreme Court he was charged with the murder of Sydney massage parlour standover man Raymond Francis Locksley. After two trials he was found not guilty in Sydney in 1984. But it was a fateful move for Flannery, who decided to try his luck in Sydney. He was befriended by notorious Sydney crime boss, the so-called 'colourful racing identity' George Freeman, who used the imported Melbourne gunman as his personal muscle.

Soon after Flannery arrived in Sydney an underworld war broke out which cost at least eight lives. During this war, Melbourne criminal Alan David Williams was involved with Flannery in the plot to kill Sydney drug squad detective, Michael Drury, who was to give evidence against Williams.

Alan Williams was a major armed robber in Melbourne in the late 1960s but in the 1970s, like many others, he moved into drugs. He began to move vast amounts of amphetamines, marijuana and heroin. At one stage he had dealers working for him in St Kilda, Elwood, Fitzroy, Williamstown, Footscray and Coburg.

'I was a giant in the trade,' Williams recalled later. 'I thought I was invincible and unpinchable.' At first he was a dealer who didn't use. Eventually he began to smoke heroin and then to inject it. He was arrested after a drug deal involving NSW undercover detective, Michael Drury, outside the Old Melbourne Hotel in 1982.

He had been introduced to the undercover man by another figure in the drug world, Brian Carl Hansen.

Desperate to keep out of jail, Williams first tried unsuccessfully to bribe Drury — and then offered $100,000 to have him killed.

On June 6, 1984, Drury was shot as he stood in his Chatswood home. He survived.

Williams' brother-in-law, Lindsay Simpson, was not so lucky. He was shot dead outside Williams' home in September 1984. It was a case of the wrong man. Dennis Bruce Allen, a vicious drug dealer, had ordered that Williams should be murdered. But the criminal he hired for the hit, Ray 'the Red Rat' Pollitt, shot Simpson by mistake.

Williams later pleaded guilty to attempting to bribe Drury and conspiracy to murder. He was released in 1992 from Goulburn Jail vowing to give up drugs and crime.

Police subsequently discovered that Flannery had agreed to kill Drury for $100,000. He took a deposit of $50,000 and stalked the policeman to the Chatswood house and shot the policeman as he stood in his kitchen washing dishes.

Drury was shot twice at point blank range, but to the amazement of his colleagues and medical staff he lived. Flannery told Williams not to bother sending the remaining $50,000 because Drury was not dead, and so the 'contract' was not fulfilled.

Flannery, who lived by the sword, was to die by it. It is believed that a group of major criminal figures decided that Flannery was a loose cannon who had to die. He disappeared on May 9, 1985. His body has never been found.

His wife, Kath, who was almost killed in an attempt on her husband, denied that he was a hitman, acknowledging only that he was 'no sugar plum fairy'.

SO much has been written on Christopher Dale Flannery, 'Mr Rentakill', and I don't want to speak ill of the dead. But really, the guy was a mental peanut with the physical courage of dishwater.

Flannery had an overblown reputation built on about 10 or 12 facts and 1,000 fairy tales. In my expert opinion he was so far behind he couldn't hear the band playing. He hated me, but the hatred was born out of pure fear.

Years ago he barricaded himself in his cell because the screw threatened to move him to cell two, side one, which just happened to be the cell next to mine. He accused the screws of trying to have him killed and demanded to see his lawyer.

The screws were only joking with him, the weak-gutted prick. But I'm glad the fag is dead.

This mental giant employed Amos 'the Witchdoctor' Atkinson, proving the man was a tactical retard. He had a close working relationship with the late 'Hopalong' Tom Ericksen. He also worked for the late George Freeman as a strongarm man, debt collector and standover man.

There are many stories about what finally happened to the bag of wind so I will tell you how he left this world. A man I believe and trust but cannot name told me the real story on Flannery.

Tough Tom Domican was the man everyone thought knocked Flannery. It was well known the two of them hated each other, so when poor old Chris went on the missing list half the Sydney underworld were whispering Tommy's name. Tom loved this. He was delighted to feed the rumours. He was not a man without an ego. In fact, he started to tell certain people that he had done the hit and had disposed of the body. But he confided to a couple of his good friends, 'I'm gonna look a nice stupe if that big prick turns up.' There was no fear of that because Tommy Domican knew that Flannery was no more. But his big mouth got him in trouble and he ended up doing time over an attempt on Flannery's life. I won't comment whether he was guilty of that or not.

Now I will tell you what really happened to Rentakill. He forgot the golden rule: trust no one, particularly if he is close to you. Flannery was hit from behind with a meat cleaver as he drove a car. The killer was a trusted ally.

I know the name of the man who did it but I will not betray him.

The man who put him on the missing list is a Melbourne-based gentleman who has put enough people on the list over the past 20 years to be believed. I would believe him before I would believe anybody in Sydney.

As for Tommy Domican, a stretch in jail should teach the Irish numbskull to keep his mouth shut and stop bragging about things he didn't do.

Flannery's body was put through a tree shredder and his minced remains rest in Seymour, Victoria. End of story.

People don't know it but there is very good mail that it was Flannery who killed Ray Chuck in the Melbourne Magistrates' Court in 1979. And he would have killed Freeman if that mob hadn't got him first. Domican was a bit player in a major production. He didn't have a starring role.

ALAN David Williams was the man who paid Chris Flannery to put a bullet into the NSW undercover policeman, Mick Drury.

I knew Williams in B Division in 1975. He was a nothing then, and in my opinion has lost ground ever since. He had a running war with Dennis Allen for a while as they blued over who would control drugs in jail. Big deal. But I'll say one thing, Williams was a cunning bastard, too bloody slippery for my liking. He was more like a fat-arsed used car salesman than a good crook. I disliked him at first sight and he knew it. He was not what I would describe as a brave man. He preferred to employ others to do his dirty work. He employed mental retards and top of the range idiots, mainly.

While it is commonly believed that Williams got Flannery to shoot Drury, I am one of the few who believe that Williams, for some unknown reason, said that to cover up the true facts and to protect a corrupt police officer. He had close links with a network of bent bobbies around the place.

I would believe very little of what came out of the mouth of Williams. He is a game player and a deal maker who operated in a world of shadows, police spies and double agents.

BRIAN Carl Hansen was a Mr Big in the drug world. He was a friend of Alan David Williams. Hansen was the man who told the undercover NSW drug squad detective, Michael Drury, that if he was a copper that he was a 'bloody dead man'.

But for all his wealth and alleged underworld power, Brian was a very frightened man. Typical of the modern drug gangster, he was without power once drugs were removed from his hands.

I personally didn't mind him as I found him no threat at all.

A guy called Tony, who was involved in the Great Bookie Robbery, introduced me to Brian. He was very nice to me ... but then again, death is always treated with respect. People like Brian being nice to me was not a sign of friendship, just of fear. Your old granny would get over him in a fight.

I wouldn't wear any of the bums on a brooch.

FLANNERY shot and killed five times more men after his death than he ever did when he was alive and well.

In matters relating to who shot who in the drug world, especially where police, honest and otherwise, are concerned, one is left with one question. What is the truth? I personally doubt that the truth has ever been told.

As far as Flannery was concerned it was a case of 'Rentafool', not 'Rentakill'. But I shouldn't be so hard on the dead, so here is my personal tribute to the man ...

THE BALLAD OF RENTAKILL

Some found him hard and cruel.
Some found him tough and scary.
But to me,
He will always be,
Just another dead sugar plum fairy.

CHAPTER 14

WHITE SLAVERS, SKINHEADS AND PINHEADS

'HE HAS NEVER DONE A DAY'S JAIL AND I
DOUBT THAT HE EVER WILL. HE IS THE
CLASSIC QUIET ACHIEVER.'

ANYBODY who thinks there is no such thing as white slavery in Australia ought to meet a guy I will call 'Milo'. Then again, perhaps they shouldn't. He's not the sort of bloke you'd want to take home to mum ... especially if you've got a sister.

Milo is an Albanian but he speaks Italian and uses an Italian name. He can't spell Ovaltine. He has no police record, but he's a top operator in the flesh for sale racket.

He runs a string of very physically beautiful callgirls. These are whores but they don't look like hookers. They are the silk department in the oldest profession. The catch is that they are slaves to Milo because he keeps them all drug-addicted ... and he sells them like cattle when he's finished with them.

The key to Milo's success is that he oversees his girls' daily drug use like a concerned doctor. He sees to it that they get vitamin injections, B12, C and E. They are kept on a programme to promote physical wellbeing: aerobics, dance classes, swimming and sun bathing. I have seen some of them and they are real glamour girls. They all look as though they are from rich families and expensive private schools.

As a cover for his caper Milo runs a small legitimate modelling agency. But the real bucks come from the top of the range escort market. All of his girls are on heroin and totally enslaved, although they seem to like their lives. But what they don't realise until it's too late is that the only way home for them is an overdose.

Milo has a few lucrative earners on the side — spin-offs from his main line of business, you might say. Because he supplies escort girls to the rich and famous, he does a nice line in blackmail. He would be making at least $1 million a year out of his beautiful but smacked-out flock of females. And I doubt, somehow, that he pays much tax.

I have met some of his girls. Heroin and bent sex is their life. Take away the needle and they would rather be dead.

Milo sends Australian girls to Asia, Bangkok and Japan and so on. After he is finished with them he sells them and they don't even know it. It is a slave trade, but as long as they are given heroin, they don't seem to realise they are being hawked like sides of beef.

The power heroin seems to have over women is greater than the physical effect on males. Of that I am sure.

THE only area of criminal activity where you still find a lot of real hard, tough bastards, the real head-banging stone killers, is in the world of the criminal arms dealer.

This is a section of the underworld that I pride myself on knowing well, although not many do. But under no circumstances will I go into great detail about the people in it. It would not be healthy.

I am talking about para-military-style criminals. The men of this world are 1,000 miles Right of Adolf Hitler. Few of them ever end up in jail. They deal in guns and they have a select group of buyers. If it is on the market they can get it — at a price — from anywhere in the world.

A gun dealer can make a major drug dealer look very tame. The heavyweights of the drug trade are girl guides compared to the arms dealer.

I have seen a man shot because he arrived at a gun sale and questioned the impact hitting power of a 9mm Glock Special. He was simply shot in the leg by way of example. He was then forced to pay for the gun, and his friends then carried him to his car.

Lesson: don't ever question the impact of a gun at a criminal arms deal. Not unless you have tin legs, anyway.

A criminal arms deal is no place for a two-bob tough guy. This is my world, and I know the men involved.

The bulk of the men involved in this world are not really part of the criminal culture. They stand in a world of their own, many of them ex-army, so Right-wing they make neo-Nazis like poor old Dane Sweetman look like a gay Commie.

One of the biggest arms dealers about is a war veteran known as Agent Orange. He is dying of cancer so he won't mind a little mention. At any rate, he owes me money so bugger him.

These men deal with the hard men of the underworld. Very little of the real good stuff ever finds its way down to the run of the mill crim.

YOU pick up a newspaper or you go to the movies and you see a million stories about the mafia. But really, in Australia, we should be far more concerned about some of our Asian friends than the boys in the black shirts and the wrap-around sunglasses.

The Vietnamese will be the next great crime wave we face in this country. There are only a few down here in Risdon Jail, but in Pentridge they are growing in numbers and are already trying to get a big slice of the action.

Physically, the Vietnamese have lost every major battle they have tried to fight inside Pentridge, but they simply never forgive and forget. They re-arm and they wait their chance to attack again and again.

The king pin of the 'slopes' in jail is a man who goes by the nickname 'Small One'. This is because he is the baby son, the fifth child in the family. 'Small One' has gained absolute power over all Vietnamese prisoners and crews inside Pentridge.

The biggest Vietnamese crime gang in Australia is Su Doan 18, the equivalent to the Chinese 14K. And 'Small One' is a leader in the gang whose influence is growing both inside and outside jail.

So far the Vietnamese have no real access to fire power, and the mainstream crims have made sure that they don't get too many guns. They have got where they have with knives, cleavers and a love of blood. However, it is as sure as eggs that they will get the weapons. Drug power and money will bring the influence and buy the hardware.

Another strong man and growing leader in the Sn Doan 18 is the man they call 'The Monkey'. I befriended him in jail and helped arm him and his bodyguard, 'The Tiger'. Both these men are known in their world as 'Sat Thu' or gunmen.

This all sounds like nonsense but the Vietnamese crime world is very serious. I see them almost as little children trying to find their way as they grow bigger and stronger. They have already learned the power and money that comes from heroin. I have told 'The Monkey' that there other ways to make it in the crime world without dealing in the powders. He is a good listener and learner. I have told him that my methods can also bring power. So remember the name of 'The Monkey' because he will become a low-profile, but much feared headhunter within the Vietnamese crime world. While the 'Small One' is the rising star in Asian crime, I think he will not live long.

Australian crime figures laugh at these little men, but they are too stupid to see that they will eventually lose their power to them. They will gain fearful power within ten years, I have no doubt about that at all.

The Su Doan 18 is also known as the 18 Divison. It has about 200 members and is growing fast. It is based in Springvale, Richmond and Footscray and has a branch at Cabramatta in Sydney.

The gang began by running protection rackets against Vietnamese shopkeepers but is now also heavily involved in prostitution, heroin, blackmail and general standover tactics. They will never stop and if the authorities don't move soon, they will become a major evil influence in Australia.

It could be worse. While the slopes are making a quid at least I can pick up some walking-around money playing Russian Roulette with them. They love gambling almost as much as they love blood, and they throw down plenty of dough to see The Chopper take a chance on blowing his brains out.

WITH all that has been written about ethnic crime it never ceases to amaze me that the so-called experts have steered away from groups who really do have a large slice of the action. The mafia in Australia has a fearsome reputation for violence and ruthlessness. It is high time this was exposed as a myth.

In mother Italy they may be strong, blowing up police, politicians and judges all over the place, but their poor gelled-up Australian cousins couldn't knock the froth off a cappuccino in a street cafe.

The police and the press watch television and read books and think the same thing must be happening here as has happened in America and Italy. When you talk of real blood and guts violence in Australia you will note the names of those involved: Flannery, the Kanes, Taylor, Twist, Bradshaw, Turner, Freeman, Smith, Cox, Minogue (Craig, not Kylie) and, of course, the old Chop Chop himself. You could toss in a few Jewish names as well, just for spice.

The Dagoes may hit the headlines, but they don't hit much else.

In the invisible empire that is called the Australian underworld the Italians count for nothing. They hold financial power and drug power, but they are not feared by anybody except Italian shopkeepers, market gardeners and grandmothers.

No, the Australian criminal world does not shake in fear at the thought of the Italian mafia. But there is an ethnic crime group in Melbourne which truly does hold the power of life and death in the underworld ... The Albanians. To be precise, a small group within the Albanian community which can strike terror into the hearts of most crims.

When it comes to death and violence this group is beyond compare. For sheer guts and love of blood, they are the tops. They have 1,000 per cent attitude towards family honour and revenge. There is no question that they have a siege mentality towards the outside world. It is interesting to note that the Russian KGB used the Albanians as hitmen and assassins.

I can say that in my time in Melbourne, the greatest friendship and loyalty I was shown came from this small and feared group. Two of my greatest and most trusted friends were Albanians.

No, it would be wrong of me to suggest that these two fine men had any connection with crime or criminals. They were just tough and honourable gentlemen who were well known and highly respected within the Albanian community.

One man is Neville Darbovski, who I simply called 'Neville the Albanian'. He was one of the bloodiest and gutsiest street fighters it has been my pleasure to know.

One of the toughest and hardest men I have known, however, was his father, Norm, a publican. He was seen as a father figure by many members of the Albanian communtity.

His loyalty and kindness to me in 1987 was given without question. I love him like my own father, and he is still in my heart.

I used to go with him to clubs in Lygon Street. It was the first time I ever saw so-called hard men kiss another man's hand and cheek. I felt like I was an extra in a Marlon Brando movie.

Norm was kind and gentle and he was always there to give advice — or money, if it was needed — to friends in need. However, I always had the feeling that if you crossed Norm, you were entering a world where suicide would be the kindest and most humane advice.

I must state that Norm and Neville were hard men but were not involved with Albanian criminals. I was happy to know that when I was out and about in Melbourne in 1987, when there were many big-mouth criminals who wanted me dead, that I had the backing of two such rock-solid types.

They showed me more guts and loyalty than I had seen in a long time. I was always able to go to the Builders Arms Hotel in Fitzroy knowing I could have a drink, a meal or even a sleep in total safety. There were many men who were frightened of Chopper Read. There were more who shook with fear at the thought of upsetting or crossing old Norm and his family, God bless them.

I mention them here as a sign of my deep respect and gratitude for the loyalty they have shown me. I have no doubt that if I had not known them in 1987, I would have been killed. They stood between me and the grave in those days and I cannot forget them.

They taught me that honest men can be hard men.

FOR some years now many and various motorcycle gangs have controlled the amphetamines, or speed, market in Australia. While they no longer have a monopoly, they are the biggest participants in the huge industry.

The bikies have cornered the market in relation to production, bringing them wealth far beyond most people's estimates. The wealth and drug power they have acquired has made them big players in the underworld.

But the rub is that these men are not cradle-to-the-grave criminals and when the shit hits the fan, the vast bulk of these so-called motorbike tough guys run for the cover of police protection. Or worse, they turn Crown witness.

There would only be a very small percentage of the members of the various clubs who could be called real tough guys. Many of the bikies are non-criminals involved in crime and this, in my opinion, is very dangerous. It is like non-medical people involving themselves in operations.

You are dealing with men who will holler copper at the first hint of trouble. I have some good friends in the bike world, but even they admit that they have a great deal of trouble with some patch-wearing members from some of the clubs.

Much of the inter-gang violence and distrust comes down to the fact that half of them spill their guts whenever they get into a police station. This results in great unrest and bloodshed between them.

I personally think that most of them have fallen off their Harleys on to their heads too often. I don't pretend to understand the political intrigue or the thinking involved, but I do know that they have great power and wealth through their involvement in drugs.

This means that they are rich, violent and weak. A senior policeman once told me that he hadn't met a bikie who wasn't prepared to talk inside a police station as long as his name was kept quiet. They are dangerous, venomous and amateurish.

Of course, there is a handful of strong men in the bike world. They know who they are and so do I. As for the rest, I piss on them. They are like overgrown boy scouts with bad attitudes. They like to run around in uniforms with patches on their back. Obviously, they should all have gone to Scotch College to get it out of their systems. You would think they would grow up.

I suppose I shouldn't try to analyse these boys. In the end, when all the talk and politics is over, a gun in the mouth is the only answer.

SOLLY is Melbourne's bonfire king. He is a torch, an arsonist who comes from a wealthy Jewish family involved in the interstate rag trade.

Solly is more a friend of Dave the Jew's than mine. He used to get around with the Surrey Road gang a bit in the old days. In the 1970s Dave the Jew and I were standing around watching a large fire when Dave said, 'Good Golly, it's Solly.' There was Solly talking to one of the firemen as Solly's mate's factory burnt to the ground.

Solly is now a millionaire involved in a legitimate business. But, so I'm told, he's still busy after hours. He is the Chopper Read of the fire insurance industry.

He has never done a day's jail and I doubt that he ever will. He is the classic quiet achiever.

READ admits to being 'Right of Genghis Khan' in matters politic. He has also been a keen observer of the small, but growing group of Right-wing criminals who call themselves neo-Nazis.

The two criminals with alleged neo-Nazi sympathies who have grabbed the public attention have been Phillip Grant Wilson and Dane Sweetman.

Wilson, a 200-cm tall giant, wanted to rule the underworld. He began a protection racket and was allegedly involved in the murders of drug couriers Lina Galea and Ricky Parr. He was involved in planning armed robberies and other crimes and had his 'soldiers' carry out the raids.

Wilson claimed to have been a mercenary in Rhodesia before setting up a factory in Melbourne. Police believe he planned to kill a Melbourne policeman by dropping him from a light plane as revenge after his best friend, Thomas Messenger, was shot dead by police during a raid on his Wantirna hosue in 1985.

Wilson was shot dead in South Yarra in August 1987. The killing has never been solved.

Dane Sweetman is not a good-looker. He was sentenced to 20 years' jail for the murder of David Noble in April 1990. The Supreme Court was told that Sweetman and another man had been celebrating Adolf Hitler's birthday when they killed Noble.

Sweetman is not eligible for release until November 18, 2005.

I'M not one for commenting on politics, as a rule. But I really must say that all these neo-Nazis getting around are in poor taste and have bad manners, and should be dealt with accordingly. And, believe me, they will be handled rather severely if they make the mistake of sticking their shaved skulls into the real crime world. The fact is that the 'Nazis' are a little bit of a sick comedy and a bad joke.

The late but not lamented Phillip Grant Wilson, the so-called 'Iceman', was one of the better-known neo-Nazi nitwits to come into the scene. He was an enforcer with the strength of a bull and the heart of a sparrow. He was a pretender: a vegetarian who ate meat, a non-drinker who drank, a white racist who loved Asian prostitutes, a man who said he hated drugs but snorted speed and smoked hash.

Wilson was a classic criminal Walter Mitty. He once spoke rudely to a mate of mine in the South Yarra Arms Hotel. I followed the big fool into the toilet and punched him repeatedly. He fell to the ground, cowering and whimpering and I relieved myself on his fallen body. He was a coward — a wet coward.

He was looked upon by the mainstream criminal world as a dangerous fool and a dreamer. The only dangerous thing about him was that he actually believed his own lies. He was involved in drugs as he wanted the money to arm his own band of Right-wing mental cases. He really did believe he was Adolf Hitler reborn. The man was in reality not a heavy thinker and he was used as a front man by others who really pulled the strings.

It was known for some time that 'Phil the Dill' was about to die. I was offered $8,000 to do it myself but the money was not forthcoming. I was also asked to get rid of the remains of Lina Galea and Rick Parr, but I refused.

It was rumoured for some time that there was police involvement in the murder of Wilson. This is something I do not believe. There were people close to Wilson who believed he was a big mouth who had served his purpose and was drawing too much attention to them.

I found out that a member of Wilson's gang had put up the money and set up Wilson. Phil had been mouthing off that this person was a police informer and that he intended to kill him. Wilson telegraphed his punches, so he got hit first.

The man who pulled the trigger on Phil is known to me and is a bit of a nitwit himself, and the price for the hit was $5,000. Set up by a junkie and killed by a semi-retard for peanuts. That about sums up how the Iceman got melted.

You'd think the other idiots would learn from what happened to Wilson. But you can't tell some of these would-be Hitlers. Pentridge has a growing neo-Nazi population — and a fool called Dane Sweetman is one of the better-known of these fools. Neo-Nazi, the way they play the game, doesn't mean Right-wing, it just means right off.

It takes more than a couple of swastikas tattooed on your body to make you a tough man. These mental pygmies march around Pentridge, poking their right arms into the air screaming 'Heil Hitler' to every bugger they see. They stick needles into their arms and they justify it because Hitler was an amphetamines freak. The two most Right-wing nations in the world, in my opinion, are Israel and South Africa. Now I am Right-wing, so Right-wing that I make these neo-Nazi nitwits look like bleeding heart liberals.

These bald baboons think it's smart to act like Nazis, but they are really just kids fantasising after watching too many ABC documentaries. Bloody halfwits.

For all I know Dane Sweetman may not be a bad chap at all but he really is a lightweight. As someone who has read *Mein Kampf*, I think it's safe to say dear old Dane wouldn't have had the mental capacity to make the short list for Uncle Adolf's SS. I think Himmler would have stuck him in a large bottle of metho and put him on display in the Heidelberg University. There are few neo-Nazis in Australia who would have read *Mein Kampf*, let alone understood it. It's pretty heavy going.

I didn't know Dane that well, but we did jail together in Pentridge's H Division in 1990 and 1991 and I know that he is a registered member of the Ku Klux Klan.

He got married in the H Division contact visit area, with his bride wearing Doc Marten boots, and the female version of neo-Nazi high fashion. I believe the marriage celebrant didn't know whether to read from the bible or *Mein Kampf*.

Dane is a bit of a fearsome-looking fellow at first sight, with his shaved head and and swastika tattoos, and he is seen by the public as a dangerous monster. But the real hard men in the system think of him and his type as an amusing comedy. Mind you, there are plenty of impressionable idiots behind bars, and he does have a small and growing following inside.

Why this fascination I don't know. Personally, I have always found the neo-Nazis to be boring and brain dead. Their only topics of conversation are Hitler and Right-wing nonsense, and the fools sucked in by the Nazi crap are just young people with nothing and no one, looking for something and someone. Hitler said that people will more readily accept a large lie than a small one and he might be right, at that. I think most politicians would secretly agree.

Ratbag political movements first stir the ratbag criminal class and work their way up. While they are no real danger at the moment, the neo-Nazis should be watched.

ONE of the favourite tricks of any self-respecting standover man is to try and get a dollar out of the trendy nightclub scene. After all, it always looks to be ripe for the picking. Lots of glitter, money, drugs. No one in that scene wants their boat to be rocked because they are making too much money.

But it is not as easy as it may first seem. The Kanes tried it in the 1970s and, after a few small victories, failed to make a mark. Others tried it and came a cropper as well.

In 1987 I had a go at it and had 100 per cent success — but I picked my targets with great care and never got greedy. But my success was only in the short term, so I suppose I failed as well.

We all try to get a piece of the action, but always from the outside. It was from the inside, from the so-called security business, that the money could be made. While the outsiders can create a stir for a short time, it is actually the security people, the old-fashioned bouncers, who control the club. And it is, of course, the security firms who control the bouncers.

Now, many of these firms are well respected and beyond reproach but some have strong underworld links. One of Melbourne's top men in the nightclub security business also acts as the personal bodyguard to an Italian underworld identity from Canton who is a major illegal gambling identity. And this security man is connected with a firm that has a piece of the action in many Melbourne nightclubs.

A big trick with some clubs is fiddling the cover charge money. While the tax man can keep his eagle eye on the bar takings the cover charge money is anyone's guess. Out of that money comes the payoffs to officials who turn a blind eye over parking, overcrowding and other matters, as well as the payoffs to certain criminal interests. Anyone who needs to be sweetened with a sly sling gets a whack out of the door takings.

This may not go on in every case, but it is widespread, believe me.

I always found that when I spoke to a nightclub owner or manager in private about the need for Chopper Insurance, they might stamp their feet and scream blue murder at first, but after a little straight talking they would see the sense in what I was saying.

After all, business is business ... and, besides, we all have to do our bit to keep money in Australia. Those nightclub owners just waste it on imported luxuries.

EVERY dog has his day, and the old underworld monster known as the Victorian Federated Ship Painters and Dockers has become a faded phantom that no longer applies in the real criminal world of today. Most of the dockers' real hard men are dead and gone and their criminal big thinkers have had second thoughts.

They still have a reputation — but that is all they have these days, and I doubt that they will re-emerge as a force on the Melbourne crime scene. I could be wrong, but I don't think I am.

I have written a poem about the decline and fall of the dockies, and it goes like this ...

> *The Kanes got it in the head,*
> *Bye bye, Brian, Les is dead,*
> *Shannon got hit with the apple cucumber,*
> *Now Pat rests in final slumber.*
> *Pat even had a bodyguard,*
> *But Machinegun Bobby wasn't trying too hard.*
> *As for Puttynose,*
> *Who can say? All we know is,*
> *He's not here today.*

Ha ha. The dockies, in my opinion, were only ever the mice who roared. Now they can't even do that.

CHAPTER 15

PSYCHOLOGY OF FEAR (OR WHY HONEST MEN GIVE ME THE CREEPS)

'WHILE MOST CRIMS WILL NOT FIGHT FOR PRIDE ALONE, AN HONEST MAN WILL DIE FOR HIS HONOUR.'

USING fear correctly is a skill, even an art. Its correct use, I believe, is to instil fear in your targets with a wink and a smile — using courtesy and a friendly, polite attitude. Only small boys and schoolgirls lose their tempers.

After all, as our mothers taught us, a spoonful of sugar helps the medicine go down. Which is another way of putting the old saying: 'Honey catches more flies than vinegar.'

I only raise my voice in anger at Mr Nibbles when he has chewed up one of my good shoes. I may lose my temper when I am trying to change a flat tyre and the jack slips. I may go red in the face when some dirty rotten greyhound or racehorse has robbed me of several thousand dollars. But I do not, as a rule, lose my temper with humans.

I will admit that on occasions I have spat the dummy towards friends who have put holes in their manners or have been acting stupidly. But I have picked it up, dusted it off and whacked it back, in a flash. I regain my self control fast.

However, in matters of business, only a fool loses his temper. Why would a man carrying a loaded gun, who is fully prepared to use it, need to be cross with anyone? The choice for the other party is clear: the money, or the rest of your life in a wheelchair. All in a nice, quiet voice.

That's why I could never rob a bank. 'Excuse me, Sir. I would like you to give me $50,000' just doesn't sound right. Somehow, it doesn't have the sense of urgency and terror that stick-up men favour in their line of work. I could never run into a bank, screaming and yelling like a drunken Indian and yip, yip, yahooing all over the place.

People don't think when they let their anger take control. I wait for the anger to subside before I act. Then I just talk to them, and their fear takes over. A frightened man is putty to control. I let them keep what they like to call their pride. I explain to them that it will be our little secret, that the rest of the world, their family and friends, need never know.

They must know that to others they remain the hero ... while at the same time paying up to me on the quiet. No business can be done unless the other party knows he will be killed if he does not comply. It is a matter of reasoning with people, but stupid human pride is my worst enemy.

In most cases, I work on a person so they don't lose face to others. There is no need to humiliate someone just to stand over them. In fact, that can be counter productive.

But it is almost as though some men demand their blood be spilled before their stupid pride will allow them to part with money. These people do not see that the money is not worth it. For them it is not business, not a simple mathematical equation. If you were to ask them in the sober light of day, what was more important, a relatively insignificant amount of money or an immense amount of pain, I'm sure they would be sensible. But some of them sometimes get hot-headed, stubborn and stupid. Then Doctor Chopper has to help them see the error of their ways.

Understanding human nature is one of the most important elements of the psychology of fear. Some men simply have to be faced with the facts; others have to face their own impending death. Each man is a complex mystery, but it seems to me that men involved in crime, who use violence as a weapon, are simple to understand. They fear pain and death more than an honest man.

This personal stupid, blind courage of honest men outweighs the personal courage of bad men. Why? Because bad men hold very little dear to their heart, whereas the honest man will often risk life and limb fighting with an intruder over a bloody television set or a video.

The bad man would not risk his neck for the life of his granny. So my psychology of fear, while it works to perfection in the world of evil men, would not work well in the world of the honest man. His righteous indignation and stupid personal pride would send him screaming to the police — or wanting to attack me with a golf putter.

You would have to kill the silly bastard just to shut him up. To be quite truthful, honest men scare the shit out of me. You just can't reason with the mad bastards. It's useless. To kill is always the last resort, but an honest man would scream so long and loud it would have to be the first resort. And where would be the profit in that?

I have a rule: never rob a 'square head'. It is not worth the fuss. To approach an honest man over matters such as this is bound to fail. Their sense of outrage dooms any such plan from the beginning. His pride takes control, this is just common sense but so many criminals fail to see it.

The criminal class has a lower sense of self esteem. It is a rough generalisation but while most crims will not fight for pride alone, an honest man will die for his honour.

There are other aspects of the psychology of fear but I cannot reveal them. Otherwise every bugger would be standing over every other bugger.

ANOTHER NIGHT'S WORK

We tied him up tight,
'Till his hands went white,
Stripped off all his clothes,
Forced water up his nose,
Full on pressure with the garden hose,
Don't touch him 'till I give the nod,
Then hit him in the neck, with the electric cattle prod,
Watch him shake, rattle and roll,
How come he drives a Merc when he's on the dole?
Give us the cash sport, and we can stop the game,
He said no, so we lit the flame.

CHAPTER 16

MAD MICKY (TANKS FOR THE MEMORIES)

'AT TIMES MICKY IS SO LAID BACK I'D THINK
HE WAS IN A COMA. BUT WHEN HE MOVES, HE
MOVES WITH PURPOSE.'

MAD Micky Marlow, or Micky Saunders, as he is also known, has been a good, loyal friend for many years.

We are, indeed, an odd couple. He is a quiet, polite fellow and a man of non-violence unless, of course, it is a matter of business.

He was born in NSW, and why he lives in Tasmania is a bit of a puzzle. He has friends on the mainland such as Peter Clune, the armed robber, and the Russell Street Bomber, Craig Minogue, who he still keeps in touch with.

Micky worked on the Melbourne waterfront in the late 1970s for a while and did a short stint in Pentridge, not that such things should be held against him. While a guest in Her Majesty's prison he had a run-in with the late Shane Goodfellow.

For reasons that I have never been able to work out, police seem to think Micky is some sort of a tank man, a safe cracker involved in criminal activity. 'Foul gossip and slander' is my reply to this sort of baseless allegation.

Some members of the Launceston CIB seem to believe that Mad Micky was the last person to see local criminal identity Tony Tanner alive. Tony vanished and his body has never been found. When I returned to Tassie in November 1991, the head of the CIB asked me if I had any knowledge of the Tanner mystery and of Micky's alleged involvement.

My answer has always been the same: Micky is too nice a fellow to be involved in such a thing. Besides, I have heard rumours that Tanner was seen drinking in a Williamstown pub, months after he vanished from Tassie.

I met Tanner in 1987 and I found him to be a disagreeable fellow with the sort of personality that is prone to suicide. The suicide factor should not, in my opinion, be ignored.

Micky is something of the local playboy and many an attractive girl has been overwhelmed by his charms. He is also a fearless punter. He once lost $13,000 in just one hour of drunken madness at the greyhounds. We play some rather foul practical jokes on each other and our methods and styles are very different.

Mad Micky is, and always will be, a loyal friend whose friendship I value. He is a thinker who will not act in haste, whereas I like to strike while the soldering iron is hot, so to speak.

At times Micky is so laid back I'd think he was in a coma. But when he moves, he moves with purpose. He has a secretive and paranoid way about him and he is always talking in a special semi-code. He is convinced that he is being followed or that his phone is being bugged.

He also has a cleanliness fetish. He is the only man I know who will spend an hour in the shower, dry himself off, and then wash his bloody hands.

Mad Micky had a falling out with my old mate, Sid Collins, and warned me that Collins was treacherous. But I thought I knew better, only to find out that Micky was correct.

Micky's motto of 'Never plead guilty' has still found him inside Risdon Jail on a few occasions over the years, but he now lives a life which has little to do with crime, other than to socialise with a few old crooks.

He is a mate and a loyal friend and has stuck on my side in spite of popular opinion. While I don't say it to his face, I am grateful for his support and friendship and I am sorry for putting holes in my manners in the name of scallywag comedy, much at poor Micky's expense.

A few crims could learn from Micky. He doesn't give people up in police stations, doesn't talk out of school and, in matters of business, is a cool-headed chap to have on your side.

Dave the Jew met Micky after the Collins shooting and both of them got on in a friendly manner, which I found strange as The Jew hates people even to see him, let alone know who he is. I have never heard The Jew say a good word about anyone since the death of Cowboy Johnny.

As anybody who read my first book knows, The Jew grew up with me and Cowboy Johnny in Prahran. He is from a wealthy family and went to Wesley College but he would have to be one of the most dangerous men in Australia. If he decides someone has to go on the missing list, that is it. He will quietly hunt them down, and then they are no more. I am always glad to know that Dave is on my side.

He is blood loyal and cold blooded. He wanted to help me with my problems in Tassie by getting rid of a few people. I told him that was not the way to go. The coppers must have heard something because they sure as hell hid away some of their witnesses in case they developed a Jewish Problem.

Micky, on the other hand, was puzzled by The Jew. He was surprised that such an ordinary-looking fellow, such a polite and gentle person, could really have such a lethal reputation.

Dave the Jew and Mad Micky have one thing in common. They are both puzzles. Complex people always are.

In 1987 Micky and myself became involved in a few matters that I am unable to write about, but let me say that Micky has been there for me when it counted. In 1987 he came to Melbourne and I introduced him to the mad drug dealer from the west of Melbourne, Scottish Steve.

It was a moment of some comedy. Before the conversation Steve suggested that we put all our guns on the table and Micky was amazed to see so many weapons plonked out in front of him.

At our second meeting at Steve's Ascot Vale house, or the house of horrors, as it was known, I witnessed the strangest conversation, with Scottish Steve talking in complete speed-ravaged, paranoid riddles and Mad Micky talking in his unique sort of code.

I was totally lost and the other two were no better. Each man left the meeting convinced the other was quite mad.

CHAPTER 17

THE RIGHT STUFF

'BIG JOE HAD MORE BLIND COURAGE THAN A
PIT BULL TERRIER ON SPEED.'

A MAN I admire greatly is G. Gordon Liddy of Watergate fame. In my view he stood for truth, justice and the American way ... his own version of it, anyway.

In some ways I condemn the Americanisation of Australia. But the Yanks have given the world some real heroes, and to me, Mr Liddy is one of the greatest. He represents strength in a man, and is prepared to bend and break a few rules, and bones, to get the job done in the name of the common good.

While the Lefty bleeding hearts of the world may condemn people like Liddy, who are they anyway? Just a pack of namby pamby nancy boys, waving their limp wrists at real men. They vomit their Lefty verbal crap, condemning anybody who has shown a bit of dash out in the real world.

G. Gordon Liddy had the capacity for blind loyalty. He was a robot soldier of the Nixon administration and did not fall to his knees in tears when the shit hit the fan. He said simply that a man should not extricate himself from a difficulty at the expense of his associates. I admire him greatly.

He was arrested over Watergate and stayed staunch through the lot. He was one of the few who didn't give anyone up. At one stage he was prepared to go and stand on an identified street corner so that he could be knocked because Watergate had failed and he was in charge. I would have thought a poor reference from the President would have been sufficient punishment, but old Gordie was made of stern stuff.

It is the way Liddy handles fear that I admire most. It's pretty well known that when he was a kid he was frightened of rats ... so he caught one and ate it to beat his fear. Thank goodness he wasn't frightened of elephants.

To show his strength of mind Liddy would put his wrist over a lit candle until you could smell the flesh burn. He is one tough man, all right. When he was locked up over Watergate a lot of black prisoners yelled out that they were going to get him. But on his way to the shower yard he started singing some old Nazi battle songs. They all decided to leave the old crazy whitey alone after that.

Liddy went on to have his own radio programme. I personally think he would make a great President. Mind you, you'd never know if he was going to wreck international relations by serving rat at the White House.

ONE of the greatest Australians now alive is the Victorian RSL President Mr Bruce Ruxton. While many people see him as a figure of some comedy, in years to come when he is in his grave, Australians will say, 'Shit, old Bruce was right.'

I have yet to disagree with a word he has said, and while a lot of

Australians see the RSL as of little or no importance, it just goes to show what short memories people have.

Regarding the topic of immigration, come the day when Australia is facing the threat of a war, think about who will fight to defend the country and who will want to leave these shores as quickly as they came.

It is not hard to see that Australia is in deep trouble, from within and from without and the 'She's sweet' attitude won't work any more. Instead of laughing at what men like Mr Ruxton have to say, we should be paying attention.

Think about it. Australia is filling up with people who have escaped one war or another and when our turn comes, they will escape from Australia just as fast.

My personal arsenal is my protection against the day this country is invaded, and I truly believe that day will come. When it does come, it's grab your guns and head for the hills time. No invading army can defeat a nation if the people of that nation are well armed and want to fight for freedom.

I've got enough heavy duty firepower and ammo stored away to hold off a small army for three months. I believe that when Australia is invaded, those who are not prepared will die ... but the buggers won't get me without a fight.

When I was a kid, like most boys, I would pretend to be out in the wild west and I would practise with my sixguns. Well, they reckon that all men are boys at heart and, in this area, I have never left my boyhood.

I will always be a devoted enemy of the anti-gun lobby. A disarmed population is a helpless population and I believe that this slow but sure move to disarm the people of Australia is a dangerous thing. A move that the people of this country will one day regret.

I will never surrender my guns.

YOU don't have to be Einstein to realise that I am a great admirer of personal courage in anybody — although I don't hand out too many wraps. And one man I greatly admire is the heavyweight boxer Joe Bugner. Some smartarse Pommy sports journalist once wrote that Joe looked like a Greek statue, but had fewer moves. To that I would just like to say that the hardest things most sports writers have ever punched is a typewriter — and even then most of them lose.

As far as I am concerned 'Aussie Joe' was the hardest fighter I have seen in the ring — not because of his boxing ability, but because he was a human punching bag who refused to lie down.

Big Joe had more blind courage than a pit bull terrier on speed. He had the brain of a scientific boxer with the heart of a slugging brawler. He seemed to punch his way nearly to the top, then get stage fright on the big night.

I really believe Joe could have been champion of the world. I won and lost a lot of money betting on Big Joe and I'd still bet that on a good day he could still go the distance with any heavyweight in the world.

He will be remembered as the heavyweight who didn't win the big one, but in my opinion he could have done it, because no one ever beat him. They may have won the fight, but they never really beat him where it counts: in his mind.

In the blind courage and sheer guts department, he will always be the real champ. Some smartarses in Australia and Britain used to bag him, but never to his face, mind you. They wouldn't be game enough for that.

I have the view that Joe was sometimes too nice in the ring. If only he had used a few more uppercuts, throat and neck punches, he could have killed his way to the title.

I suspect he was the victim of poor advice, training and management in his early career. A lot of trainers are fantastic at showing the little blokes what to do, but are lost when they get to train a heavyweight.

I know how I would have handled Joe's training. My strategy would have been not to fight to win by a knockout or a TKO: we would fight to kill.

Forget about spilling your own blood, or the points your opponent might get, and aim for the side of the neck, uppercut with the left, then try to smash his windpipe and snap his neck. Corpses don't win fights.

Think murder, because it is legal in the ring. And at least if you don't kill him, you'll win the fight.

Aussie Joe could have done it. He had more guts than God. He will always be my boxing hero.

I think I would have been a great boxing trainer. Any pug who beat my boy would be running a big chance of copping a double barrel in the car park.

CHAPTER 18

TONE-DEAF KIDNAPPER HITS WRONG NOTE

'MR EASTWOOD DID NOT ARRIVE AT
PENTRIDGE ON A WAVE OF POPULARITY.'

EDWIN John Eastwood is one of the most notorious criminals in Australia.

Eastwood was jailed for 15 years for kidnapping six school children and their teacher, Miss Mary Gibbs, from the Faraday Primary School, near Bendigo, in 1972. Five years later he escaped from Geelong Jail and kidnapped nine children and seven adults from the Wooreen Primary School.

Eastwood demanded a ransom of $7 million and was shot in the leg and recaptured after a high speed car chase with police. He was sentenced to 21 years for the second kidnapping.

In 1979 Eastwood completed a religious course run by the Seventh Day Adventist Church, in 1982 he did a bible study course and in 1985 he was baptised in jail. But religion didn't stop him getting into trouble: in 1981 he was charged and acquitted of killing standover man Glen Joseph Davies in Jika Jika.

In 1990 he was released on parole but was convicted of a factory burglary, sentenced to 12 months and had his parole revoked.

In Read's first book he said he felt that Eastwood had reformed and would not commit any further crimes when he was eventually released again.

Read described him as a 'true gentleman, and a loyal friend'. However, Read did write that Eastwood loved to play the guitar and that he drove other inmates crazy by strumming the instrument for hours. 'What we had was a tone-deaf kidnapper with visions of taking to the stage one day. The first stage out of town, I was hoping.'

Here the kidnapper replies:

Dear Mark,

I recently received a letter from a reporter asking me to comment on various aspects to do with you.

I just thought I would let you know that I won't be replying to him as I don't wish to have anything to do with you ever again in any manner, shape or form.

I read in utter disbelief the personal attack you made upon me in your book. I am pretty naive, I guess. I thought we were on reasonably good terms and yet you turned on me in your book with lies, just like a snake.

I have done what you have always suggested that I do and have written a book of my own, due for release soon. When I read your book it took me three weeks to remove all I intended to say about the Mark I thought I knew and replace it with a smaller summary of the Mark you obviously are.

Your book has obviously taken priority over everything in your life to the point of sickness. I look back now on that day in H Division labour yard when you tried to snap my neck.

I realise now, with sadness, that you sought to take my life, not through the slightest hint of real malice, but merely as something that would make good subject matter for your future book. I left that incident out of my book merely out of respect for the good side of you that you seem so keen to stifle.

I wish you well for your sequel, but I want to make it quite clear that I don't want to have anything to do with you ever again. With mates like you, who needs enemies?

Do yourself a favour and seek psychiatric help.

Ted.

WHEN I received this letter from my old mate, 'Tedwood', Ted Eastwood, I could tell he was not at all pleased with me. The only thing I said about Ted in my book was a comical reference to his musical ability.

Like so many crims, Ted can tend to take himself a little seriously and he sees his ability with the guitar as something akin to Eric Clapton.

I don't remember ever mentioning my nearly snapping his neck in a playful wrestling match in H Division. Perhaps I should also mention that if I had wanted to snap his neck, purely in self defence mind you, it would have been heard all the way to Faraday.

Ted also forgets to mention that his friendship with me, many years ago, kept him alive for a long time. If I may be crude enough to bring up the past, Ted is, in fact, the kidnapper of small children — not once, but twice. Let me assure you, therefore, that Mr Eastwood did not arrive at Pentridge on a wave of popularity. His friendship with me helped keep his neck in one piece and it certainly didn't do anything for my popularity.

I suppose I must now sadly admit our friendship is over. For the life of me, I still can't work out what I said to offend the poor bugger.

Even so, it must be said poor Ted still can't play the guitar.

PS: I did go to the psychiatrist once, and when I went to leave the doctor said, 'Send in Ted Eastwood.'

Ha, ha.

CHAPTER 19

THE PRINCE OF PAIN (OR WHY I HATE DENTISTS)

'HE BROKE SEVERAL TEETH, THEN DUG IN
LIKE A WELSH COAL MINER.'

A TRAINED observer might notice that I have half the teeth missing from the top of my mouth. This is a little memento of a visit I had to a prison dentist in the 1980s. I use the term 'dentist' loosely. The man is no longer there and I cannot remember his name, but if he was to walk over to me in a pub and introduce himself, I would not be responsible for my actions. And after hearing the full story I don't think any jury in the world would convict me. In fact, I am sure they would find that it was a clear-cut case of justifiable homicide.

This dentist was a man with a weak wrist, he was not physically strong and he had a nervous disposition. I suppose looking inside the gobs of psychopaths didn't help his mental state.

I went to see him in handcuffs. Personally, I thought they had the cuffs on the wrong bloke. I still don't know why he was nervous. Surely, it wasn't the crack that I didn't like dentists, that I wanted any treatment to be fast and painless, and if it wasn't I would be forced to do something rash. It was only a joke, but he turned pale and gave a nervous laugh.

While he was giving me one of four injections he dropped his syringe on the floor, picked it up, and said with a little giggle, 'nothing broken' and then put it back in my mouth. There would have been something broken if I could have got my hands free, I can assure you.

I knew I was in terrible trouble. He pulled 11 teeth, three from the bottom back and the rest from the top — and he only injected the top.

He had trouble with each one. He broke several teeth, then dug in like a Welsh coal miner. I said as I pulled his hand away, spitting blood on the floor, 'Are you a real dentist?' I was sure he had broken my jaw. He had one knee on my chest and the other on a chair to get leverage.

The prison officer guarding me screwed his face up as he saw what was happening. My jaw felt as though it had been dislocated for several months. I will remember that man's face until the day that I die. He would have been a great asset to any torture gang. A gas bottle blowtorch or the boltcutters pale in comparison. That man was the Prince of Pain.

DUE to the lamentable lack of bar service at Pentridge, I was often forced to enjoy a drop of aftershave and coke. A cheap bottle of aftershave and an icy cold can of coke.

I would fill up a cup of aftershave then down it really quick and chase it down with half a can of cold coke. It got you roaring mad drunk in about 90 seconds, fighting drunk in my case. But it did give you sweet smelling breath, even if it did cream off half your brain cells.

It was a dangerous and desperate drink and I would not recommend it. I put some very large holes in my manners under the insane influence of aftershave and coke. It really is the devil's brew, believe me.

In Jika Jika we used to get large, very cheap bottles of some floral-smelling French afershave, made in Hong Kong. But for special occasions we might crack a bottle of Brut or Old Spice. The top shelf, a cheeky little drop with a good nose. Ha ha.

JEFF Lapidos is a well-meaning bloke who heads the Prison Reform Group. He was the head of the Prisoners' Action Group, but there was a split and now there are two groups.

What these people do is a mystery to me, but both groups love to hate The Chopper, which is a never-ending source of amusement to me. Lapidos and his motley collection of do-gooders have a radio programme on community radio. When I was in Pentridge, I would hear my good name mentioned on the programme regularly. Some of them seemed to hate me with such venom that it was comical.

While the do-gooders desperately want to help some of the inmates, the amount of prisoner support in jail for them is very slight. A small group of malcontents worship Lapidos and they would want him as their president after 'the revolution'. But the vast majority of prisoners see it all as a giant yawn.

The Vietnamese can't understand the prison reformers and the neo-Nazis don't like them because some scallywag told them Lapidos was supposed to be Jewish. The rest of the jail population are too drugged out to even listen to the radio, leaving the reformers to deal with a small group with political aspirations. That mob would think Mao Tse Tung was a Chinese brand name for one-minute noodles in a cup.

I see Lapidos as a harmless Lefty. Peter Reid, who was acquitted of the Russell Street bombing, thinks the world of him.

WHEN it comes to Pentridge, one fellow I must mention is Henry. I will not mention his real name because of legal concerns. I have known

Henry for some 20 years. We have been in the same divisions over the years and never a cross word has passed between us.

I have been disgusted over the past three decades to see the hard men of the crime world over-run by drug-running wimps, but Henry stands out as the exception, one of the few who will not change his ways.

You won't see any big stories about him but he is one of the quiet, hard men of the criminal world and the prison system. He would rather do someone a good turn than a bad one. Yet I know that he is a very violent man when he is crossed, or in matters of criminal business.

Henry is from the old school and wouldn't give anyone up. He didn't try to involve himself in the politics of the prison system and the various power struggles. And he doesn't involve himself in underworld feuds on the outside. He has always been desperate to keep a low profile, but I have seen him upend some of the biggest gangsters about, much to my amusement and delight.

He is a fair dinkum tough man and although we are not close friends, I have always liked his style.

MY first book has brought all the criminal whackos out of the woodwork. Once upon a time, all prisoners dreamt of escaping ... now they dream of best sellers. Jails all over Australia are humming to the sound of typewriters and word processers as assorted nitwits, junkies and lunchtime legends pound out their life stories and their tales of woe.

Ted 'call me Eric Clapton' Eastwood is writing his life story. I understand my old sparring partner, Keithy Faure, is writing his story. And the Hoddle Street killer, Julian 'pass the ammo' Knight, is writing his memoirs. And these are just the sane ones.

Well, there has been a book done on Walsh Street. And I suppose there will be one on Russell Street, Hoddle Street and Queen Street as well. As for the rest of the mental retards, if they have to they should all get together and combine their life stories ... they could call it *Sesame Street for Psychos*. My God, what have I started, having mentioned these retards in my book. They now want to write their stories.

So it has come to this: from gang wars to publishing wars. Like it or not, I'll win this war too. Keep banging away, you pack of dream merchants.

THE LUNCHTIME LEGENDS

He's the lunchtime legend from a gangster comic,
The man who could not lose,
The boss of all bosses, who got his guts from booze;
He hasn't got a story, so he'll tell a heap of lies,
A man of broken dreams, he goes to his cell and cries.
He could never beat the Chopper, none of them ever could,
He's got the mind of a rat but the heart of a plastic hood,
So now with his typewriter he plots his big reply,
None of them could beat me, or make me fall and die,
Face to face, I beat the lot; all it took was a dirty look,
So now he plans his comeback, the nitwit is writing a book.
Well, I hope he goes real well, and gives it a real good burst.
But just remember, arse wipe,
The Chopper got there first.

CHAPTER 20

THE BEACH BALL DIDN'T DO IT

'HE KILLED A TURK ONE DAY WITH JUST ONE
PUNCH, AND HE WAS FOUND NOT GUILTY.'

IN October, 1991, Read's close friend in H Division, Frankie Waghorn, was convicted of the murder of smalltime drug dealer John Turner, 41.

The Supreme Court was told that Waghorn and another man repeatedly stabbed Turner as the victim pleaded for his life.

The court was told that the pair stole Turner's jewellery, valued at $10,000, before burying the body in a backyard rubbish heap.

Waghorn shared the house with Turner before the murder.

The Crown alleged that a woman in a nearby bedroom heard Turner say, 'Please no, there must be some other way'.

An autopsy showed that Turner was stabbed 38 times in the head and chest. The woman said she heard a voice say, 'Give me your knife; these other knives are breaking.'

Waghorn was convicted of the murder, but he appealed and won a retrial. He was convicted again at the second trial and sentenced to 17 years with a minimum of 13.

I HAVE mentioned that one of the few men who has stuck with me is Frankie Waghorn, the big bald beach ball who, I reckon, could punch the teeth out of an elephant. I have said before that the number of sooks in jail who cry that they are innocent can be numbered in their thousands. They all say they were innocent but there would only be a couple I have ever met who have a legitimate case.

Now Frankie may be a mate, but let me say that I believe that Frankie is one of the few who can rightly claim he has been hard done by. I know for a fact that Frankie had nothing to do with the murder of that two-bob junkie gangster, Johnny 'Beeper' Turner.

Far be it from me to speak ill of the dead, but Turner was a junkie, a bigmouth and a rat. And they were his good points.

His only claim to fame was that he was the nephew of the old-time heavy Joey Turner. Big deal. Joey was only a fetch and carry boy for a big-time crook called Jack Twist.

If Frankie Waghorn had backhanded Johnny Turner, then Turner would have been in a coma. Frankie could stop a raging rhino with a left hook. Frankie has never needed weapons; he is the last of the true bare-knuckle men. The hardest puncher I have ever seen, he is bloody deadly with a punch in the mouth.

He killed a Turk one day with just one punch, and he was found not guilty. To think that Frankie Waghorn would need to repeatedly use a knife in order to kill a physical flea like Turner is laughable.

Frankie Waghorn is doing life over this rubbish and I will scream long and loud that he is not guilty.

Junkie false pretenders told lies about him and he got life. Frankie is no angel. He is a crook, but whatever he has been guilty of, he did not kill Johnny Turner, believe me.

He is the only truly innocent man convicted of murder that I know. Mind you, if you listen to blokes inside, there's not a guilty man in any jail in Australia.

MAYBE Johnny Jones could tell the real story. Johnny Jones is a two-bob thug and crim who had big dreams of being a tough guy until the spoon and needle got the better of him.

He has done time for various crimes of violence, including a manslaughter charge where he buried the victim in the backyard. Now he is doing a life sentence over the murder of Johnny Turner. Surprise, surprise, Turner was also buried in the backyard — but this time at Frankie Waghorn's house.

Both Turner and Jones were house guests at Frankie's. Jones got arrested on an armed robbery charge, then asked for bail and promised that he would tell police about a murder. He then told them that Frankie Waghorn had put Turner off.

After several changed statements and assorted stories, Jones was charged with murder, but he wanted to bring Frankie along for the ride.

Jones is now in strict protection in Pentridge because if Frankie tosses just one punch at him it will be lights out forever, believe me. Jones is just another example of how drugs can pervert, corrupt and destroy the very soul of a man.

In return for trying to help Jones and Turner and trying to get them off drugs, all Frankie got was cruel betrayal.

FRANKIE

Frankie got the lot,
So tell me why and for what,
Pinched on a set-up murder blue,
What was said in court wasn't true,
Yes, I know he's not a saint, and he's no wimpy cupid,
But he's too bloody smart to have been so bloody stupid,
Frankie's not a mug, or some two-bob learner,
And I know for a fact, he never put off Turner.

CHAPTER 21

HOPALONG TOM, THE SNAKE WITH ONE LEG

'HE PLAYED ALL OF US LIKE A VIOLIN.'

ONE-legged private investigator Tom Ericksen was a master of living in the shadowy world between the police and the underworld.

In the 1950s Ericksen, the son and grandson of policemen, was an insurance salesman who sold policies to members of the force.

He then became a private detective and debt collector, and was the leading repossession agent of a major credit firm.

Ericksen made a number of contacts with junior police who were struggling on poor wages. He employed them during their days off to work in the repossession game.

Some of them went on to take senior positions in the force in the 1970s and 1980s. Ericksen was a master at attempting to exploit his past relationships with these men.

Another man he employed at the time was Gianfranco Tizzoni, the man involved in the murders of anti-drugs campaigner Donald Mackay and dope dealers, Isabel and Douglas Wilson. Tizzoni later turned 'supergrass' and informed on mafia boss, Bob Trimbole.

Both Ericksen and Tizzoni carried documentation giving them authority to act for the now defunct Federal Narcotics Bureau. Ericksen acted as a bodyguard for a well-known Melbourne lawyer in the 1960s.

He loved mystery and used electronic gear in a bid to compromise people he thought could be exploited. He once used a Melbourne lawyer in a bid to set up one of the top detectives in the state.

He bugged the lawyer's chambers in the hope of recording the policeman making admissions which could be used against him. The bid failed because no admissions were made.

Ericksen kept a dirt file, where every scrap of information about prominent people in the criminal justice system was kept to be used against them, and he traded information between police and criminals. He claimed to have major contacts with the PLO and Libyan agents and travelled the world, claiming to be a diplomat or an ambassador. He often used a Hutt River Province passport to move between countries.

Ericksen used Melbourne hitman Christopher Dale Flannery as his muscle, and once used the paid killer to methodically bash a city retailer in his Exhibition Street office.

After Flannery disappeared in 1985, Ericksen began to lose his influence. He was targeted by the National Crime Authority in Operation 'Viper' and was charged with 195 counts of giving secret commissions and 11 charges of making threats to kill.

But he didn't live to stand trial. He died a blind diabetic with heart disease, in August 1988. He was 52.

'HOPALONG' Tom Ericksen was a private investigator with a wooden leg, a lot of enemies and some friends in high places. I was approached to kill him in 1987. I gave it some serious thought and planned to plant a series of jumping jack mines along his driveway. I had the gear to do it but the deal became complicated because of the people involved.

I was supposed to be paid $250,000 for the hit. The price seemed like bullshit and when there was no deposit coming I got suspicious. I don't knock people on credit.

Then certain police advised me to steer clear of the whole episode. Even men with no ears must learn when to listen and this was one of those times.

Anyone who got involved with Tom, friend or foe, was dancing up the road of insanity. Even police involved in trying to convict him ended up half paranoid. Nothing about Ericksen could be believed.

He was the perfect conman, because he believed his own lies. He acted in a manner which suggested that he was some sort of secret agent. He told me he not only had PLO connections but was on side with the IRA and had done work for the outlawed Italian secret society, P2.

Tom was the master of disinformation and played the police and the underworld off against each other. Alice in Wonderland lived in a world of total reality compared with Tommy, believe me.

The police had a code name for him, they called him 'The Viper'. Funny name, that. I've never seen a snake with a wooden leg. The underworld had another name for him: 'The Riddler'.

I am now told about the contract I was supposed to take to kill Tommy, that in fact he was the man behind it because he wanted an attempt on his life as part of some mysterious mind game. He was a dangerous Walter Mitty of the highest order. His favourite bedtime reading was Sherlock Holmes, James Bond and other thrillers that he tried to turn into real life.

Tom made a small fortune through his trickery and protected it in a world of paranoia, suspicion and intrigue with the cops and crooks dancing like puppets.

Chris Flannery and Ericksen were close for some time. Ericksen convinced Flannery he had high government connections. In his personal diary he carried the number of the CIA in Washington and Virginia. But the truth is he got them out of the American telephone books.

I agreed to be a witness for him against the National Crime Authority. He and I had agreed on a number of matters and I sent Margaret to see him. The bloke had a mini-tape recorder inside his wooden leg. As I look back on it there is no doubt that 'Hopalong Tom' was a complete nutter, and a dangerous one.

There must be a host of criminal figures, high-ranking police and a few media people who must cringe with embarrassment to think they ever got involved with 'Hopalong'. I must include myself in that, as he played all of us like a violin.

THROUGHOUT the years I have been dealt with and confronted by and questioned by all manner of police — state, federal and the National Crime Authority, the Victoria Police internal security unit, the Federal Police internal investigation division and various state and federal task forces. And, in my experience, I must confess that the most paranoid and secretive outfit was the NCA.

I was questioned by the NCA in relation to my involvement with Tom Ericksen. On each visit to the NCA I noticed that they tended to speak in riddles — in a sort of code. I will give a classic example of NCA-speak.

'Hi, Chopper. Well, we don't have to tell you what this is about.'

To which I would say, 'No. What do you want to know?' And they would answer something like 'It's about the one-legged bloke. You know. T.E.'

'Oh, yeah,' I would answer.

Then the NCA bloke would say, 'Well, we know what's going on. What we want to know is why you're putting your head in.'

'My head in what?' I would say.

'Well, it's been on TV that you've been paid to kill him, and we know you're in touch with him and that you've been involved with him for years. So what's the go with the court case? What are you getting out of it?'

'What the hell are you on about?' I asked.

'We know you're going on his side against us,' they would say. 'We know what Tommy's up to.'

By this time I was getting peeved. 'So what do you want to talk to me about?' I said.

'We are just letting you know it won't work, and we can't offer you a deal. But if you come good on this our way, we can whisper in a few ears. You know how it goes. Don't worry. We won't somersault you. All we want to know is what Tom's game is. Which way he intends to jump.'

To which I replied, 'All I'm willing to say, gentlemen, is that I was approached by two men who I now know to be NCA informers in relation to me killing Tom Ericksen, and I knocked the approach back.'

'Look, if you side with Ericksen, you'll lose. We have him on the PLO thing. We have him on tax. We have him all the way. Introducing you to discredit our witnesses won't work. But if you're willing to walk away, wipe Tom, lose your memory and tell him to piss off ... well, you know.'

I said, 'Well, I know what?'

'Well, one hand washes the other. Strings can be pulled. How much is Tom paying you?'

By this stage I had a bloody headache. After three visits I was totally confused as their double talk and riddles became more scrambled. Then Tom died — and I got a letter from the NCA saying 'We can't help you.'

I never asked them for their bloody help. The NCA lived in a world of their own. Total insanity.

My agreeing to be a witness for Ericksen against the NCA could have created big problems for me. As a police force the NCA was a dangerous comedy. They lived and acted like paranoid spies, confusing themselves and everyone else ... and Ericksen was twice as mad. With him in one ear and the NCA in the other it was unbelievable.

They spoke in riddles and code in case they were being bugged. Meanwhile, they were bugging me. It was total comedy. I must add that dealing with 'Hopalong' Tommy would have sent any policeman a touch mental. I wasn't sorry to see him die. Had he not ended up dying I probably would have ended up shooting the old trickster myself. Ha ha.

CHAPTER 22

RENEE, A HARD ACT TO COPY

'I FOUND HER TO BE A SASSY LITTLE THING
WITH A LOT OF SPUNK.'

I REMEMBER Frank Sinatra once describing the Australian press as a pack of whores and liars. Who am I to argue with the great Cranky Frankie, the Don Vito of the musical world? Well, maybe I disagree with him just a little bit about some people in the media business.

Before my first trial over the Collins shooting I received a lovely letter from Renee Brack of the *Hard Copy* programme from Channel 10, wishing me all the best for my court case.

I had done an interview for *Hard Copy* with Renee and I found her to be a sassy little thing with a lot of spunk. When this skinny little girl bounced up to me at the Launceston Airport, I am ashamed to say that I was gripped by the overpowering urge to pull her on like a wet, soapy sock. However, good manners, and the fear that I would almost certainly be stabbed to death by Margaret, held me in check.

Renee proved to be a hands-on reporter, eager to have a go at shooting with the infamous 'hole-in-the-head' shooting club. She took to firearms like a duck to water.

She wouldn't weigh more than eight stone soaking wet in an army overcoat with bricks in the pocket, but she has a heart as big as Phar Lap's — and a much better figure. I was most impressed with the girl's guts. She was prepared to fire the .357 magnum and even the pump-action shotgun. She was a natural, and if she ever needs a gun she knows where to come.

She had dash, and was far from the wimpy 'care for another pink gin' brigade that I have encountered in the past. People with guts in the television world are few and far between, in my opinion.

Being the gentleman I am at all times with the fairer sex, my desire to please Renee and give her a good story backfired on me a little bit. They shot some footage of me playing Russian Roulette with a .357 magnum. I was pissed during the filming, and in my experience Russian Roulette and drunks do not mix.

Renee wanted some good footage, so after convincing her that the gun was unloaded I put it to my head and pulled the trigger. I then put it to her head and pulled the trigger.

She nearly fainted, but it was all just a joke. Or so I thought at the time. The *real* joke was that after the camera was turned off I re-checked the weapon and pulled the trigger twice, pointing the gun at the ground. It went off. The bloody thing was loaded after all, with one shell and five empty chambers.

The cameraman asked whether it had been loaded all the time, and I said, 'What do you think I am, stupid?' But I was bluffing, don't worry about that. The truth was, if I had pulled the trigger twice more while the barrel was pointing at Renee's head, it would have been all over for her. It would have been great for TV, but not so great a career move for Renee.

The worst thing is, I bet *Hard Copy* would have used the footage ... I would have got life, but they would have got an award. And they reckon the underworld is unscrupulous. But seriously, I still don't think Renee knows how lucky she is to be alive.

I had a look at all the footage and I realise now that by trying to give them some good TV I condemned myself out of my own stupid mouth. The Crown has the footage and tried to use it in the first trial. I would have come over as a right mental case, which would be most unfortunate for the grandson of a Seventh Day Adventist bishop. You could say the gunplay filmed by *Hard Copy* was good for ratings, bad for courtrooms.

After seeing the footage I wrote to the Tasmanian DPP, Mr Damian Bugg, and informed him I was prepared to plead guilty to the charge of being too good-looking in a public place.

In the end, they were not allowed to run the footage in the courtroom. The funny thing is that, during the filming, Renee wanted to know if I could show I was a good shot. To show her I'm not just a pretty face, young Trent Anthony held out a stubby of beer and I shot it from a fair distance away. It exploded everywhere and apparently looked pretty dramatic on TV.

Funny how things turn out. In the end, it was Trent who was a key witness against me. Hindsight is a wonderful thing. I don't think Trent would fancy holding any stubbies for me these days.

Renee was meant to be a witness for the Crown in the first trial, but the Crown must have decided she would be more my way than theirs and so they didn't call her. But they tried to use part of her interview with me on *Hard Copy* against me. They also tried to use part of the book against me, even though the jury was not allowed to read it.

Renee wrote again wishing me the best for the second trial. So, in spite of Frank Sinatra's opinion of Aussie journalists, I can say that at least one of them is a mature, gutsy, good-hearted woman who was fun to meet.

Who's Frank Sinatra, anyway? Just another singing Dago. I've never had much time for the mafia and all that 'Godfather' crap. The only horse's heads that have ever worried me have been on beaten favourites.

CHAPTER 23

WHO'S WHO IN BLUE

'THE PROFESSIONAL POLICEMAN AND THE
PROFESSIONAL CRIMINAL: THERE IS NOT A
LOT TO SEPARATE THEM.'

OVER the years I have had a funny relationship with the police. Some of them think I'm a dangerous psycho and they might be half right; I certainly can be dangerous: just ask anybody who knew Sammy the Turk and a few other blokes who are no longer with us. There are plenty of police who think I'm trouble and have steered well clear of me. They belong to a new generation of lawmen who are a little wet behind the ears when it comes to true blood and guts crims. The closest they come to a 'real' gangster is when they hire an Arnold Schwarzenegger movie from the video shop.

The trend is that more and more police no longer associate with crims because they are frightened people will think they are up to no good. But it wasn't that long ago that you could have a few drinks with a few cops who knew who was up who and why. You could have a laugh, share a bit of mail and walk away happy.

In fact, there are a few people walking around now who would have been put on the missing list by my good self if the police had not had a quiet word to me on the sly and said it would not be in my best interests to give these particular citizens the lime funeral.

No lawyers, no courtroom dramas, just a quiet word over a few beers. There's a few dockies they would have scraped off the ceiling with a putty knife if the cops hadn't had a quiet word into where my ears used to be.

But the cops these days are frightened that if they are seen with a crook, people will think they are on the take. They are more at home looking into a computer screen, calling up records, or studying 'flow charts' than looking a crook in his beady eyes.

My attitude to police is mixed. I dislike weak people, stupid people and two-bob, false pretenders. I am sad to see that while the criminal world is starting to overflow with would-be junkie gangsters. The police are also going backwards.

To my mind, police forces around this country are tipping over with young, over-educated nitwits who can't see the wood for the trees. They could hardly be trusted to look after a children's crossing, let alone investigate and solve serious crime. They have no idea how to deal with people or the art of man-management.

Physical courage is foreign to many of these younger police. With their higher education, they look down their nose at the old-style bone breakers. And so, in my opinion, the tough hard men of the police force are being pushed out and replaced by the 'thought police'.

The shiny new young men in blue like to spend all their time thinking and talking about how to solve crime, but they actually haven't a clue of how to go about it. When I see these earnest young insects, I just shake my head.

But all is not lost. There are still a few cops about with the dash to get out and mix it. Some are tough, some are bad and a few are just mad. Not all that different, really, to some of the hard case crims they're after. The professional policeman and the professional criminal: there is not a lot to separate the two. By a professional cop, I mean a career policeman, and by a professional crim, I mean a career crook. It is their life; they know no other.

Police find it difficult, in a social context, to mix with and talk to people other than police. And criminals, real criminals, spend their time with other hard crims. While the two groups don't often mix socially, they talk a lot about the same things.

I've heard police talk for hours about the many and various criminal identities they have either arrested, investigated or done legal battle with in the courts. On the other side of the fence, I have heard crooks talking about big-name police identities they have matched wits with. There is a heap of black humour in conversations from both groups.

Believe it or not, there is a grudging mutual admiration between the two groups. I can enjoy the conversation of either ... God only knows what the shitkickers talk about.

OVER the years I have met a few coppers for whom I have a bit of respect. Here's a few I've met — and some I wouldn't want to meet again.

Cedric Netto

CEDRIC Netto is a well-respected senior Australian Federal policeman. He has served with the National Crime Authority and the now defunct Joint Task Force. In 1992 he was transferred as Superintendent, Drug Unit, Canberra.

THERE is one high-ranking policeman in the Federal Police Force I don't mind. His name is Cedric Netto and I first met him when he came out to Pentridge for a chat some years ago in relation to the Walter Mitty-type private investigator, 'Hopalong' Tom Ericksen.

Now, unlike the movies and books, I have found that most 100 per cent honest policemen are a dull and boring lot with little mental ability and little to say for themselves. They have the level of imagination and the mental agility of fruit bats. Cedric, who was obviously honest, was one of the few exceptions to the rule. He was honest to the point of being sickening — but he was so mentally alert that it was frightening.

Cedric was with the NCA when he came to see me and we have bumped into each other a few times since. Each time it has been a case of 'Hail fellow, well met'.

We had mutual respect ... he thought I was a psychopath, and I reckoned he was the most cunning copper I'd ever met. I'm glad he's not stationed in Tassie.

Inspector Garry Schipper

INSPECTOR Garry Schipper is considered by many to be the strongest man in the Victoria Police. He first came into contact with Read when the policeman was stationed at Kew. Read was aged about 15 at the time and the giant policeman left a lasting impression. Schipper went to the armed robbery squad and the breaking squad. He was later promoted to Inspector and transferred to Prahran.

MY old mate, big Garry Schipper, is one of the few police I really respect and personally like. It is not socially acceptable for a crim to actually be friends with a cop, but in my heart I like big Garry. I always have and always will, as I have known him since I was 15 years old and he was a young cop.

Raymond Chandler wrote about a character called Moose Molloy that he was 'a big man — but no wider than a beer truck and no taller than a double storey building', or something like that. I don't know who Moose Molloy was, but if they make another film of that book, Big Garry gets my vote for the job. Garry is a very big man indeed: six foot six in the old money, weighing at least 20 stone, with the strength of a bull and the courage of a pit bull to go with it.

Garry is close to a legend in the Melbourne criminal world. And the bottom line of the legend is that he is a man best left alone. He is a cop whom it is wise not to upset. He's like a sleeping bear ... it is best if one tiptoes past without disturbing him.

During the Beach Inquiry, big Garry was given a hard time over alleged heavy-handed tactics during questioning. Nonsense, I say. I don't believe a word of it. Garry is too nice a guy for such shenanigans. He wouldn't hurt anyone, unless, of course, they got between him and the dinner table. To me, he will always be one of the few real, hard but fair coppers I know. A gentle giant, tough as guts but with a heart of gold. A class of cop that is fast disappearing from the modern police force.

Despite his kind nature, Garry is also in my opinion the hardest copper I've ever met, capable of instilling respect with sheer force of personality. His word is trusted, his promises are kept. If you cross him, it is a most unwise career move.

While I never feared Big Garry, I considered myself fortunate not to be on the big fellow's 'shit list'. He only ever spoke to me regarding criminal matters a few times — and I 'pulled up', seeing the wisdom of Big Garry's words.

A policeman does not earn respect by popping on his uniform. Like all men, they have to earn respect. And I respect Big Garry.

Incidentally, Garry is also a handy yachtsman, regularly taking part in the Sydney to Hobart and other national and international yachting events.

Detective Inspector Rod Porter

DETECTIVE *Inspector Rod Porter has had two stints with the armed robbery squad. In a 20-year career he has also served in the St Kilda uniform and CIB branches, at Collingwood police station and with the Bureau of Criminal Intelligence. In 1992 he was stationed at the Crime Co-ordinator's Office.*

'ROCKET" Rod Porter is one cop I got to know quite well in recent years. When I got out of jail in 1986 I became involved with a few members of the armed robbery squad, and he was one of them. You must remember I had been in jail a long time so I wasn't too choosy about the company I kept.

We would go to the Fawkner Club Hotel near the St Kilda Road police station and have a few good sessions. We had mutual enemies and I was prepared to co-operate with them over certain matters. They were investigating a few people I didn't like and, after all, an enemy of my enemies is my friend.

I found 'Rocket' to be a most agreeable fellow. A touch wary, but I don't hold that against him. After all, any policeman meeting Chopper Read after dark would have to be a touch mad to begin with.

He was not mad, but maybe the demands of the job make some detectives seem a bit eccentric to outsiders. In my opinion, anyone who worked in the armed robbery squad for long and was still 100 per cent sane deserves a medal. 'Rocket' is honest. He would never take a bribe or do anything to be ashamed of. But there was a reckless bravery about him which I found frightening.

Rod was a risk taker and he had a unique sense of poetic justice. One night after a few drinks Rod supplied me with a bulletproof vest for my own protection. Hours later I shot dead Sammy the Turk (drug dealer

Siam Ozerkam) outside Bojangles Nightclub in St Kilda.

It was a Melbourne winter's night so maybe the police gave me the jacket so that I wouldn't catch a cold. Most considerate.

After I was charged with the murder I made a number of serious allegations against some police, including 'Rocket' Rod.

But in the end I was found not guilty of murder because the jury believed my version of self defence. I understand Rod was most annoyed that he was investigated after I made a few statements, but in the end nothing came of it and everyone lived happily ever after (except Sammy, of course).

Making allegations was all part of the game at the time and there was nothing personal in it. I sincerely wish Rod Porter all the best. He was — and is — a good bloke. But somehow I doubt whether we'll ever have a good session at the Fawkner Club again. Pity.

Detective Sergeant Stephen Curnow

DETECTIVE Sergeant Stephen Curnow has been a long-serving armed robbery squad detective. Well-liked and thorough, Curnow has also worked at the St Kilda station.

STEVE 'Dirty Larry' Curnow can give the impression that he is barking mad; but you'd be smart not to be conned by this act. He is pretty cunning when he had his mind set on it. And he's got a bit of dash, but I hope he never gets a police valour award from the Queen because he can be a bit on the rough side and would be a certainty to upset etiquette at Buckingham Palace.

Steve was an eating and drinking machine. In between swallows he would gulp down food, then try and hold a conversation: eating, drinking and burping at the same time.

In my humble opinion, he had the table manners of a goat and the social graces of a jackhammer, but a great sense of humour. He gave me a lift to Margaret's house in Collingwood once and when I got out of the car, my false teeth fell out of my shirt pocket. Now, I was proud of those teeth as I had a half-carat diamond set in one of the front ones. But that didn't worry Larry ... he took off laughing and ran over Chopper's choppers.

A class act. What he lacked in grace he made up for in suicidal guts. He was a hard man not to like.

Barry Hahnel

BARRY Hahnel was a Senior Detective in the armed robbery squad, later promoted to Sergeant at the City West station. He was convicted in 1991 of attempting to pervert the course of justice and sentenced to four years' prison with a minimum of 18 months.

BARRY 'The Boy' Hahnel was a young cop I met with 'Rocket' Rod Porter and Steve 'Dirty Larry' Curnow. I first met him in 1987 at the Fawkner Club. The first couple of times I met him he was a quiet young man, and butter wouldn't melt in his mouth.

He was a wide-eyed, blond-haired, innocent sort of young bloke, new to the armed robbery squad, and at that time he lacked the cynicism and the pot belly of some of his older colleagues.

But by the third time I had met Barry he was swaggering through the hotel door like Al Capone's brother-in-law. I suspect that living up to the image of his heavyweight mates in the squad turned his head a little bit.

Don't get me wrong, he may have wanted to live up to the image, but it wasn't bluff; underneath it all he was genuinely tough. He was in the thick of it and didn't take any backward steps. He was there during the arrest of Russell 'Mad Dog' Cox and I thought he would go up the police ladder, as he had a good education.

It wasn't to be. It turns out senior police took a dim view of Barry's gung-ho tactics and he landed in hot water. I was a touch sad to learn that he copped a jail sentence because, win, lose or draw, he was a tough young bugger and he had guts. What more can you say in any man's favour.

Detective Superintendent Allan Pleitner

THE head of the Bureau of Criminal Intelligence, Detective Superintendent Allan Pleitner, ran into Read more than once. Pleitner remembers him as a hard case who always had a joke to tell, even when he knew he was about to be charged with a serious offence. 'He was quite a character,' he said. Pleitner, 30-year veteran of the force, worked in the homicide, consorting, arson and drug squads, as well as extensive uniformed service, before taking over the BCI.

I HAVE not been shown much kindness in my life, so I can remember nearly every time someone has done the right thing by me. As most people with a passing knowledge of the underworld scene would know, in 1978 I tried to abduct Judge Martin from the County Court in a hare-brained attempt to get my old mate Jimmy Loughnan out of jail.

One of the cops who grabbed me was Detective Sergeant Allan Pleitner. I think he was in the Consorting Squad at that time. I was off my head. I had just recently cut my ears off and I was deeply mentally disturbed.

I remember Mr Pleitner. He was very thoughtful and kind at the time. I think he was one of the police who escorted me to the Magistrates' Court. I never forgot his kindly attitude to someone a lot of people would have regarded as a dangerous psychopath and I was pleased when he was promoted to take over the arson squad.

When I went into the homicide squad to be charged with murder over the Sammy the Turk episode, Mr Pleitner must have been relieving officer in charge of the squad at the time. He stepped in front of me in front of all the other police, put out his hand and with a big smile said, 'How are you, Mark?'

We shook hands and after I was charged he let me ring my dad in Tassie. It mightn't sound much, but these little things stick in your mind. Many coppers aren't worth a second mention but Allan Pleitner is one from the old school, hard but fair.

Senior Sergeant Merv Pickering

SENIOR Sergeant Merv Pickering was the President of the Victoria Police Association. He was a policeman for more than 30 years, working in the crime cars and the District Support Group. He retired in 1990.

BIG Merv Pickering was another giant of a man, one of the old-style coppers who ruled Greville Sreet, Prahran, with an iron fist. He once questioned me over three stabbings in Cromwell Road, South Yarra, and while I confessed nothing, I was glad when the interview was over.

I believe a mutual respect grew between us and what began as an angry and ugly meeting ended with a little trust. There should be more coppers like big Merv. Tough, hard, yet with the old-fashioned Aussie sense of fair play. In a world full of very forgettable coppers, he still stands out in my memory.

Chief Inspector Allan Taylor

ONE *of the interesting CIB identities in the Victoria Police Force was Chief Inspector Allan Taylor. This interesting older-style policeman retired as head of the crime squads in the 1980s.*

ANOTHER old-time copper was Chief Inspector Allan 'Diamond Jim' Taylor who, I think, had been an armed robbery squad detective. My dad introduced me to him when I was only 11 or 12 years old. I remember looking up and thinking what a giant he was. Years later I bumped into him again; it was 1979 and I was going to court, yet again, over some trivial matter of violence.

I was suprised to realise that he no longer seemed a giant. He was in fact about the same height as me, or maybe a whisker shorter. He didn't need to be a giant to be a good copper.

'Diamond Jim' was respected and a little bit feared in the underworld for his thinking ability. He had a great 'catch 'em and convict 'em' rate and he didn't rely on physical force. He was cunning and shrewd, and there aren't many to match him these days.

Fred Silvester

FRED *Silvester was a young English bobby who decided to come to Australia on the toss of a coin in 1949. Many criminals and a few politicians wished he had bought a return ticket. Silvester was part of a team that exposed organised illegal betting cartels in the 1950s. He was one of the first Australian policemen to warn the public about the dangers of organised crime. He was the first head of the Victorian Bureau of Criminal Intelligence and the first Director of the Australian Bureau of Criminal Intelligence. He retired with the rank of Assistant Commissioner in 1983.*

FRED Silvester was not a copper I had anything to do with, but among the hard old crims, like Horatio Morris, Billy 'The Texan' Longley, Vincent Villeroy and even Reggie Kane, his name was often mentioned.

I first heard his name when I was 15. He was respected and feared, not for violence or physical force, but for his thinking ability. He had a reputation as a clever copper who spent his time gathering evidence against you for at least six months before he would even bother to speak to you.

Some of the old heavies said he was more the Scotland Yard type of copper than the Russell Street CIB variety. It was generally believed that if 'Scotland Yard Fred' was on your case, sooner or later you were going to jail. It was all done in a cold, hard, businesslike manner.

He was feared but, oddly enough, not hated.

Cops today want to be *Miami Vice* clones. Like a lot of young would-be crooks, they watch too much American television. Instead of being flash idiots they would be better off learning from the 'Scotland Yard' types who are far more feared by the underworld. The only crook I ever heard speak ill of Silvester was a domestic killer, and he didn't count, as he wasn't a real crim.

Most detectives shouldn't have that title, because they don't really detect. They tend to rely on informers, they want to be told what is happening and they can therefore be manipulated.

Men who can solve a crime without the benefit of an informer are rare indeed. Silvester had that reputation.

Senior Sergeant Brian Murphy

TALK to any criminal or policeman in Victoria about Detective Senior Sergeant Brian Murphy and you will get an opinion. 'Colourful' would be

about the safest description. Murphy was known for his courage, contacts
and eccentricity. He tended to run his own race. No one seemed to know
where he would pop up next. In 1971 he was charged with manslaughter
after Neil Stanley Collingburn suffered fatal injuries in the Russell Street
police station. Murphy and another policeman were acquitted of the charge.
Murphy retired in 1987.

THERE was only one policeman whose name could strike fear into most crims in the Melbourne underworld — Brian Francis Murphy.

Brian wasn't a big man and he was as bald as an egg, but he was a man to steer away from if you had even half a choice in the matter.

The old 'bald eagle' is a living legend in Melbourne police and criminal circles. He got his respect and reputation through what could diplomatically be called 'force of personality'. Let's just say that I did not go out of my way to get into his way, and I believe that Murphy had the same attitude towards me.

I believe he treated me as someone best left alone, provided I didn't rock his personal boat. And let me tell you, I had no intention of even going near his wharf, let alone his boat.

It was rumoured for many years that the Kane brothers and 'Putty Nose' Nicholls acted as informers for Murphy. The truth will never be known unless Murphy himself wishes to confess, and I somehow think that is unlikely. Mind you, if he did decide to put his memoirs together, it would make *Silence Of The Lambs* look like a bedtime story, and sell like beer at a wharfies' picnic.

The truth about Murphy is that while he might have picked up information from Nicholls and the rest, he was also well respected by the other side in the dockie war, including my old friend, Billy 'The Texan' Longley.

I could never work out how Murphy, and only Murphy, seemed to

Above: Sid Collins's house … not bad for a retired bikie.

Middle: The Ford I gave Trent Anthony.

Left: Sid Collins's driveway … the place where, he claimed at first, he was shot from 'a passing car'.

Above: Tasmania's Anita Betts … as good as Col Lovitt, QC, but better looking.

Left: *Hard Copy* reporter Renee Brack … has guts, loves guns.

Former Detective Senior Sergeant Brian Murphy taking care of a baby … no truth in the rumour that the kid 'fessed to three stickups.

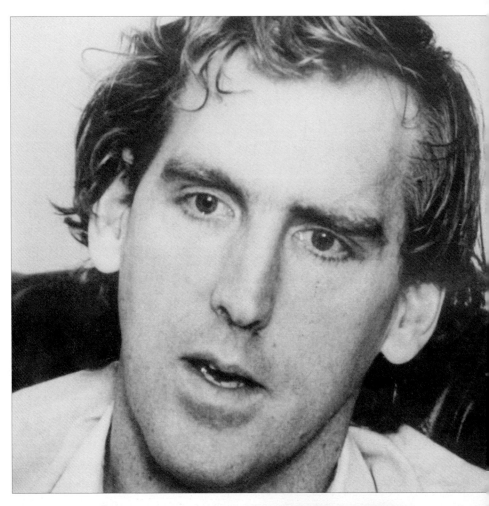

Above: 'Big Phil' Wilson … neo-Nazi, standover man, drug dealer, and dead. It didn't happen for him.

Left: Dane Sweetman … another right-wing fruitcake. Thinks Sieg Heil is German for 'taxi!'

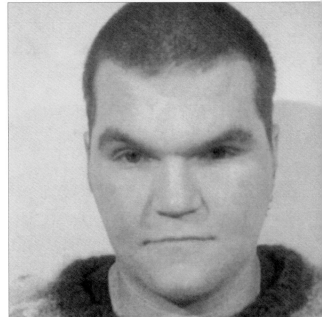

Above: Protecting our backs … me and Big Josh Burling.

Below: Guns and poses … the hole in the head shooting club meets again.

Two sides of Margaret … a day at the races (*below*) and a day out with da boys (*above*)

ig Garry Schipper: top cop, but not to be trifled with, especially at meal times.

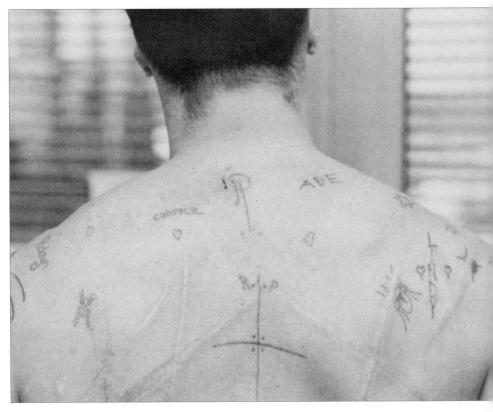

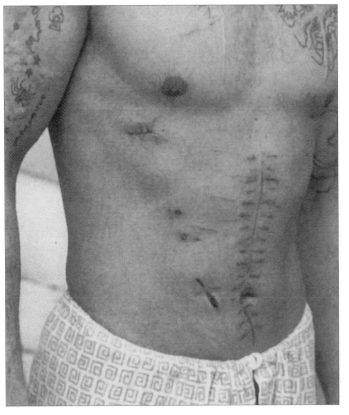

The legacy of a lifetime at the sharp end of crime. The burns on my arm are from taking off tattoos with a blowtorch. My advice: read about the underworld, but leave it at that. It's no joke.

be able to keep up friendly associations with both sides of the fence. I can only put it down to that famous forceful personality.

Longley once told me that in the late 1960s Murphy parked his car down at the docks while he was talking to Dougie Sproule and Putty Nose. Some young dockies who didn't know better broke into his car and stole his nice new golf clubs. Now, Murphy was not happy about this. He had words with Nicholls, and suggested it would be best if he got his golf clubs back. He was left in no doubt of Murphy's anger. He had the clubs back within days. It's London to a brick on that it was the first and only time hot property was ever returned at the docks.

But there was more to Murphy than his impeccable contacts on the waterfront and elsewhere. The Bald Eagle was an odd bird indeed. For sheer blind guts and rat shifty cunning, he could never be found wanting. One thing was for sure, even some of his 'friends' feared him. He stood alone.

He retired a few years ago, untouched and unbeaten, an absolute legend. One interesting thing about him was that for a man who didn't mind mixing it with some of the worst crims about, Murphy was very churchy. He was raised a strict Catholic, and it is said he was more frightened of an angry priest than 100 angry crims. He only had to see a priest or a nun half a mile away and he'd take his bloody hat off.

THE SKULL

Murphy was the master of the bullshit and the baffle,
He'd be in anything from a gunfight to a raffle,
From a gunbutt to a headbutt, he dropped a hundred men,
He'd fight 'em till they couldn't stand,
Then he'd do it all again,
He loved to go a round or two,

CHOPPER 2

This tough old Melbourne Jack,
He lost his golf clubs down the docks,
But by God, he got them back,
Love him, or hate him, they could never call him dull,
A bloody Melbourne legend,
Was the cop they called 'The Skull'.

CHAPTER 24

WHO'S WHO IN THE ZOO II

'JOCKEY SMITH HAD A REPUTATION AS A
TIGHTWAD ... A MAN WHO COULD HAVE A
HUNDRED GRAND UNDER THE BED AND GO
OUT AND PINCH A RUBBISH BIN.'

Greg Smith

GREGORY *John Peter Smith was an armed robber with a difference. He went to a private school — Parade College, Bundoora — but left early to get a job in a factory.*

He married and became a father while still a teenager. He went back to school, graduated, and then went to Melbourne University. Older than most of the students he became a campus radical leader. His Left-wing politics, good looks and charisma made him a popular figure. He was involved in using and selling marijuana as part of the student culture. But later Smith became a heavy heroin user and needed money, desperately. He began to rob building societies and stores. He became known as the 'Building Society Bandit' and was eventually charged with 26 counts of armed robbery, despite a total haul of only $38,000.

Smith was sentenced to 23 years' jail, later reduced to 16. He was outraged. He felt he had been given a sentence longer than a killer could expect.

In 1980, Smith escaped from Pentridge and for the next ten years lived the life of a drug-crazed thrill seeker. He spent his time travelling through India, Asia and Europe, was connected with the Sri Lankan Tamil Tigers terrorist group and helped the Afghanistan rebels in their war.

Eventually, after several close calls, Smith was arrested in Frankfurt, Germany carrying 272 grams of heroin. He was extradited to Melbourne and returned to Pentridge Prison, from where he had escaped more than a decade before.

IN relation to Greg 'Doc' Smith, he was a jail friend and was also a maniac junkie. I first met him in the cells of the Supreme Court in 1978 after I attacked Judge Martin in the County Court.

Greg Smith came from an upper-middle-class family and was an educated fellow who could speak several languages. He also had a black belt in karate. I found him to be a posh sort of crook, and, even though he wanted to punch heroin into his arm, I quite liked the guy.

He'd had some St John's medical training and got the nickname Doc as a result of saving the lives of assorted junkies who had overdosed.

I received some assorted postcards from him now and again, from Germany, France, Italy, Spain, India and London, just signed Greg, 'Doc' or 'travelling man'.

We had heard that while he was on the run he had worked as a volunteer medic for the freedom fighters in Afghanistan. Nothing would surprise me with him. When he came back to Pentridge after some 11 years on the run, he had an accent from speaking foreign tongues for so long.

Greg threw his arms around me in the H Division laundry and greeted me like a long-lost brother.

He had tears in his eyes. It was good to see him. He is an ultra smart, gentle-natured, almost loving man and it is very hard not to like him. What can I say? His story and his adventures would fill volumes.

Greg once told me he had a drug problem. 'I just can't get enough of the stuff.'

Stephen Sellers

STEPHEN Donald Sellers was a safe breaker, bank robber, drug dealer and extortionist. He was also a bad driver.

Sellers was one of the main witnesses in the Beach Inquiry into the Victorian police in 1976. Police were criticised in the inquiry for accidentally pushing Sellers from a third-floor flat in South Yarra. In 1979, he was blasted with a shotgun as he answered a telephone call in a motel in South Yarra.

In 1988, he was killed when the car he was driving left the road and hit a tree near Orbost in far-eastern Victoria.

STEVE Sellers was a well-known criminal until he ran into a bit of bad luck — and a gumtree — when his car crashed in the bush between Melbourne and Sydney.

Steve was popular and a feared big-money gangster with a giant reputation. His arch enemy in the Victorian police force was Big Garry Schipper. But I wasn't a wrap for Sellers either, which is how I came to almost drown him in a massage parlour bubble bath.

I had known Sellers off and on during the 1970s, but it was in this particular St Kilda massage parlour that I really got to know him. I was standing over the parlour at the time and, being young and foolish, I fell for the trick of agreeing to come back and collect the money later. You don't have to be told: when I went back to the place to pick up the cash I found someone waiting for me. It was Steve Sellers, and he was extremely angry.

The fight was fast and furious, and we found ourselves falling into a large, soapy, hot bubble bath. Whereupon, I thought it wasteful not to take the God-given opportunity to hold silly Stephen's head under the water for quite a long while.

When the bubbles stopped coming out of his mouth and when he stopped struggling I dragged him out. He must have swallowed half the bathwater. Two ladies wearing high heels, worried looks and not much else saved his life with mouth to mouth and all that first aid business. Steve spewed up soapy water and vomit and coughed and gasped and spluttered. It was all very embarrassing from his point of view, and funny from my point of view. I've seen some funny sights in massage parlours, but this was a classic.

Sellers might have come off second best with me — and that gumtree — but while he was around he was considered a sharp operator by some. He had more moves than a chess board when it came to making a dishonest dollar. He was involved in blackmail using both prostitutes and homosexuals, and was known in the criminal word as a 'poof rorter'.

In fact, it was widely known Sellers was involved in some sort of relationship with a prominent member of one of Melbourne's grand old retailing families. This chap was a millionaire and a homosexual and was supposed to be in love with Sellers and to have put up a lot of 'dark money' to back Sellers' ventures into the Melbourne massage parlour scene. Sellers and his millionaire were often seen together, and when Sellers fell out with him the millionaire shot himself. Call it a lovers' tiff.

Incidentally, Sellers' paranoid hatred of the policeman Garry

Schipper dated back to the Beach Inquiry, when he gave evidence against Big Garry. Personally, as I have written elsewhere, I have always liked Garry. While it is not quite the done thing for a copper and a crook to be matey, I suspect had it not been for our different career paths we could have been good friends.

All in all, I'm just as happy that it was Sellers who pranged his car, and Big Garry who didn't.

John Palmer

JOHN William Palmer has a feared reputation as a strongman in the Victorian underworld. He was involved in the armed robbery of the Car-O-Tel motel in St Kilda in 1974 where two men were murdered. Barry Robert Quinn was convicted of the double murder. Quinn himself was murdered in Pentridge in 1984 when he was set on fire by another inmate.

Palmer was convicted over rapes and sentenced to 13 years. He was released in 1986, but later arrested and convicted of nine armed robberies in the northern suburbs and sentenced to 12 years' jail. The court was told he had committed the armed robberies because he was a drug addict.

For more than five years from 1975 Palmer and Read were at war in Pentridge after Palmer claimed Chopper had eaten all the sausages for the H Division Christmas dinner.

JOHN William Palmer, nicknamed 'Piggy' Palmer, came from an old painter and docker family. In the 1970s he was a young, rising star on the Melbourne criminal scene, earning himself a feared reputation as a gunman and standover man.

The key to Palmer was that he couldn't fight which made him even more dangerous with a gun in his hand. He was a basher of prostitutes and did all his fighting with a gun. He stood behind an army of loyal friends and hangers-on, who fought all his fights when Palmer found himself in jail. The cherry on top of the cake reputation-wise was when Palmer was acquitted on the Car-O-Tel motel murders in St Kilda, the crime of which Barry Quinn was convicted.

It was Palmer who really started the war with me in Pentridge and then stood back and allowed Keithy Faure to fight his fight for him resulting in the five-year bloodbath that became known as the 'Overcoat War'. Faure now looks upon Palmer as gutless human filth. Palmer's last bodyguard in jail was Paul Brough, who died of a drug overdose in 1987 after some shifty scallywag handed him some pure heroin. Drug addicts are dead easy to kill. It could be called 'self-inflicted murder', and it is the perfect crime. Agatha Christie would turn in her grave because drugs have taken all the mystery out of murder.

I once saw Palmer bash an old man in the D Division remand yard with a scrubbing brush. He turned into a violent and vicious sadist when he had a weak and helpless enemy. Little did he know that day that his turn was coming ...

Palmer is one man I never killed who I should have, and not killing him has been a constant source of regret on my part. However, what goes around, comes around ... drugs and the needle have driven the once-rising criminal star to the very bottom of the ladder. The beginning of the end for Piggy came in 1977 in the H Division number one shower yard, when at last I got my hands on him. Without going into the details, he left the shower yard in tears.

John Dixon-Jenkins

A GOOD friend of Read's while in jail was the so-called 'Anti-Nuclear Warrior', John Dixon-Jenkins.

Dixon-Jenkins was sentenced to 12 years' jail in 1991 over kidnapping seven people in Bendigo Jail. He was extradited from the US to face the charges after he had jumped bail while on a world lecture tour.

He was sentenced to six years' jail in 1984 over a series of bomb hoaxes he'd made in Melbourne to highlight the peace cause.

He has told friends he will die in custody.

MY old mate John Dixon-Jenkins is at it again, demanding a humane death and to be allowed to die for peace. He writes to anyone he can think of to express his views. If he doesn't get what he wants then he says he will have a prolonged hunger strike until he dies, poor chap.

I think what worries him most is not the state of prison food but the state of the USSR or whatever it's called now. With the break-up of the Soviet Union there seems to be little or no immediate threat of the nuclear holocaust, and this has really kicked the arse out of the old anti-nuclear warrior. The world has seen the end of the cold war and the nuclear threat is no longer a problem, so where does that leave an old anti-nuclear campaigner? Up shit creek without a fission rod. Ha ha.

While I do like old John, the poor fellow is barking mad, that much is quite obvious. But he is a serious man, and any threat he makes should be treated seriously. Bless him.

Jockey Smith

JAMES Edward 'Jockey' Smith was one of the big name armed robbers of the 1970s. Uncompromising and cold blooded, he was eventually considered to be public enemy number one. Smith, born in Geelong, was involved in stick-ups in Melbourne and Sydney. He once escaped from Pentridge using a borrowed visitor's pass.

Smith was arrested in Sydney as a suspect for the murder of a bookmaker,

Lloyd Tidmarsh. When Smith was approached by police he produced a .38 revolver and attempted to shoot Detective Inspector Robert Godden. Godden lunged and stuck his thumb between the hammer and the firing pin before the gun discharged.

Smith was convicted of the attempted murder of the policeman. He was released from jail in February 1992, and shot three times two days later. He lived.

THE death of the Kanes tore the arse out of one half of the criminal world, while the death of Ray Chuck tore the arse out of the other half. For some reason men like Russell Cox and James Edward 'Jockey' Smith worked better while 'Chuckles' was around. Not a lot has been heard about Jockey Smith in quite a few years, but in his day he was the bank robber's bank robber.

It was one of Jimmy Loughnan's proudest boasts, before he died in the big Pentridge fire of 1987, that for a short time he worked with Jockey in the 'banking business'. Loughnan would re-tell some very funny stories about Jockey, and judging from similar stories from men who also worked with Jockey I think it is safe to say that while Jockey was a top mechanic in the banking business — one who had amassed and lost several fortunes — he had a reputation as a tightwad ... a man who could have a hundred grand under the bed and go out and pinch a rubbish bin rather than pay cash for it.

Ray Chuck described Jockey as a top bloke 'but not a great one for dusting the cobwebs off his wallet'. In fact, he reckoned Jockey would bite the head off a shilling, he was so tight. But in the armed robbers' hall of fame Jockey Smith is a living legend. The big money bank robbing crews are gone and almost forgotten, and so Jockey Smith is becoming a memory of the past.

Bank robbery was once a highly skilled occupation. However, the junkies tore the arse out of that. Now every needle freak with a stocking mask is in on the act.

Peter Croft

PETER Croft was former amateur heavyweight boxing champion and something of a scallywag in the Melbourne underworld. I say 'something' because the truth is he was more a drunk and a punch merchant than a crook. However, he did get mixed up with, and broke the law with, some big-name crooks. He was great mates with Russell Cox and Ray Chuck, to name a couple of big names, and there were others. Peter's only problem was he thought that in time of trouble his enemies would put on the gloves and hop into the ring with him. He got himself badly shot up as a result of this attitude.

Peter was a good-natured bloke, if a bit on the slow side — a touch punch drunk, in my opinion — but I liked him. In the early 1970s (I forget the exact year, but not because I'm punch drunk) Peter gave me and Cowboy Johnny Harris a lift in his cherry red Ford Falcon GT about 10.30 one night. He took off up St Kilda Road at 110 miles an hour — blind drunk — then put his head out the driver's window and proceeded to vomit. He had both hands on the wheel, and his big ugly foot flat to the floor. There was nothing we could do. My whole life passed before my eyes. It was a truly frightening experience.

Peter is dead now. He was a memorable fellow, in his way. He did a lot of jail time, but I never considered him a real cradle to the grave criminal. He was more a drunken, fun-loving madman, easily led by his so-called friends.

During the 1970s, a great many boxing title holders ended up involved in crime and in prison. 'Kid Billy', a former Australian lightweight champ who was a well-known crim's brother, did time in

Pentridge in that era. And he had plenty of mates in there who had gone a round or two for a pound or two.

Lance Chee

LANCE Chee was one of the gang who robbed a Clifton Hill bank in 1976 where off-duty police officer Michael Pratt was shot. Chee was not involved in the shooting as he fled out the back door. He was sentenced to 15 years for his involvement in the robbery. In 1983, he escaped while visiting his sick grandmother in North Fitzroy. He was later recaptured and released in the later 1980s. Michael Pratt was awarded the George Cross for bravery in his attempts to stop the robbery.

LANCE Chee is a bloke who has been around for a long time. He is an old-time crook, but with few, if any, of the old-time criminal codes or morals running through him.

He used to run around with Keithy Faure. However, during the Overcoat War he left Faure to fight alone.

Chee is another legend in his own lunchtime. A heavyweight amongst the limp-wristed junkie, gangster set. If you wear a dress, you could be in danger of a belt in the mouth, but as for the rest of the criminal world, Lance Chee is no threat whatsoever.

I am left totally puzzled as to how men like Lance Chee achieve their reputations. I mean, who has he ever beaten? Who has he ever shot? It is another mystery to me. Yet, believe it or not, he is a feared and respected criminal identity in Melbourne.

Pass the bucket. I feel sick.

Bustling Barry

ANOTHER Melbourne criminal I remember well is Bustling Barry. I got to know him in Geelong Jail in 1984.

Bazza and I walked into the shower room to find a young man performing a sordid act on a well-known crim. I said, 'Cut that shit out, you pair of poofters,' but they carried on as if it was a perfectly normal activity.

Barry kicked the young bloke under the jaw — not a full hard kick, but a solid boot all the same. Then both parties started to scream, with blood everywhere. One had a fractured jaw, and the other, a badly bitten dicky bird. Neither man told the authorities what had happened. I will not tolerate that sort of behaviour in my presence.

Barry must have a thing about dicky birds. A karate expert attacked him once, and in the middle of a flying kick, Barry pulled the trigger on his 12-gauge shotgun, blowing his attacker's personal parts to bits. Self defence, but, if I may say so, a touch heavy handed.

Shane Goodfellow

ON June 12, 1987, Mark Brandon Read shot dead a drug dealer, Siam 'Sammy the Turk' Ozerkam, in the car park of the St Kilda nightclub, Bojangles. He was wearing a bulletproof vest provided by detectives at the time. Several witnesses were called at Read's murder trial. Among them was an old enemy, Shane Goodfellow, who was at Bojangles that night. The jury elected to believe Read's story that the killing was a clear-cut case of self defence. Goodfellow died of a drug overdose in 1992.

SHANE Goodfellow is dead. He went against me as a Crown witness in my murder trial over the Turk outside Bojangles.

Goodfellow, as I have said before, was a top crim, a violent streetfighter with a massive reputation as an up and comer, and there were no real signs that he would be stopped.

He was known as 'Hollywood' throughout the 1970s. There was no more feared streetfighter than him. His reputation for violence was horrific. There were few better than him in his day. There were some who were more violent, but few had his reputation. He and one of his mates were a streetfighting double act that demanded fear and respect and got it.

In 1979, Goodfellow and myself crossed swords in the H Division shower yards and it saw him up-ended and covered in his own blood for the first time.

In the incident in the shower yard, I punched ten shades of shit out of him — but he was still a man. You see, I cheated. I attacked the poor bugger while he was putting his pants on after he got out of the shower. But if people want fair play, they should join a cricket club.

Goodfellow took his bloody defeat well. Not a word of abuse or a threat followed. He took it on the chin with grace and style. He said it was his own fault: 'I shouldn't have turned my back on the sneaky bugger.' He feared no man. He was also solid and would not talk in a police station. He made no complaint over our fight in the shower yard. He wouldn't dream of it. He lived by the sword, and if he fell on it now and again, that's the way it went.

Shane could have been anything within the criminal world, but he fell to drugs. Heroin in the arm did what no man could to 'Hollywood'. It took his dignity.

From being a feared streetfighter he turned into a lackey for two-bob gangster drug dealers.

Scum that Shane would once have spat on gave him orders. They held him in check and controlled him. He was under the control of heroin and it was sad to see. From legend to lackey; it made me sick to watch it. So when he gave evidence against me in the murder trial it was because drugs had destroyed his sense of criminal honour. But I must add that if anyone who ever went to trial had a Crown witness against them like Shane Goodfellow, no one would ever be convicted. Ha ha.

He was a tough man, but then the drugs got hold of him and he started the slow, pathetic decline that so many like him have suffered. I have mixed feelings about his death as I remember him as the man he was, before drugs.

However, an enemy is an enemy, and a dead enemy is wonderful news. As I have said many times before, the one who wins the game is the one who lives the longest.

All I want to do is outlive my enemies. All I want out of life is to have the last laugh. So to Shane, what can I say but ... ha, ha.

Jimmy Reimers

JIMMY Reimers and I grew up together in Prahran, and went to the Turana boys' home together. We have known each other for a long time. We were always friendly, but we went our separate ways. He became good friends with my worthy adversary Keithy Faure and the man who turned informer on me, Shane Goodfellow.

I am sad to say that Jimmy got into the heroin and the needle. He backed Keithy against me in the great Overcoat War in Pentridge. We were in B and H Divisions together and also spent some time in Jika Jika.

When I gave it to Goodfellow in the H Division shower yard, Jimmy had to get a smack as well. But for some reason, we always remembered our past. Prahran and the boys' home: we had been through too much together to become blood enemies.

Jimmy ended up waking up about a lot of his so-called friends. But it was too late.

He is a knockabout crook who isn't frightened of violence, and no one could doubt his guts. He got shot in the neck at St Vincent's Hospital trying to escape. He was a young gunman who was on his way up until the smack got him.

We liked each other a lot as kids, and youthful memories are hard to shake. But he went his way and I went mine. It is too late to say it now, but if Jimmy had stuck with me, he would have been much better off.

Lionel the Lip

THERE are more ways to kill a cat than by choking it with cream ... and more ways to make money from crime than by pointing guns at people or lighting up the old blowtorch under their toes. Something the public doesn't hear much about are the conmen who have made a career of touching people for big amounts of money. Everyone knows the film *The Sting*, with Paul Newman and Robert Redford, but not many realise there are smarties right here in Australia every bit as cagey as the Henry Gondorff character played by Newman in the film.

It was never really my line of work, but I always take an interest in other people's trades, and one of the best in the con business in Australia was a gentlemanly old chap called Lionel the Lip.

Lionel, bless his heart, was an old man even when I first met him. I was 17 years old and he was well into his 60s, so I reckon he would be dead now ... unless he talked God into extending his time on this side of the pearly gates, which is a chance, as Lionel was nothing if not a good talker. In fact, as a trickster and confidence man, Lionel was considered one of the best to draw breath or a dud cheque. A kind-looking, well-mannered old gent, he specialised in giving the impression that he was a wealthy farmer, grazier, land owner, horse breeder, cattleman, gold mine owner or gem dealer. He looked like someone's nice old uncle down from the bush — but he was old bird and had as much larceny in him as Long Bay. Or maybe more.

Lionel mostly worked the country circuit, regional cities and mining areas. He was a great student of human nature, and that was the secret of his success. He told me that the only person easier to trick than an honest man is a dishonest one. He taught me that the golden rule of every con is greed and getting the other bloke to believe that he is taking advantage of you.

Like I say, it wasn't exactly my line — but he taught me some things about human nature I won't forget. He was an old gent, a non-violent man, who worked using physical appearance and verbal banter as weapons. A master of his craft, he had a better practical grasp of applied psychology than a university full of shrinks.

Donny the Don

DONNY is Australia's oldest and foremost safe cracker. The man is a craftsman and has been the pupil master of Australia's leading younger 'tank' men.

From a key lock to a time lock, Donny the Don has cracked them all. He was caught a few times in his younger days, as a result of being informed on, or just through sheer bad luck. But he has never faced a tank he couldn't open.

Donny was an old-time crook — non-violent, quiet, a gentleman criminal from the old school.

I understand that when Jimmy the Toecutter was approached re torturing Donny the Don for his money, he was appalled at the suggestion. Jimmy said that Donny was an old gent and a master and that he would not consider lifting a hand against him.

Bob Dix

BOB *Dix was the secretary of the Victorian Branch of the Federated Ships Painters and Dockers Union. He was thrust into the limelight as a defender of his members during the Costigan Royal Commission into organised crime. Dix died of natural causes in 1988.*

I GREW up in the days when the Painters and Dockers were a feared force. But I was to learn over the years that most of that reputation was built on drunken yarns with old men in pubs around Port Melbourne, Prahran and inner suburban areas.

One of the leaders of the dockies in those days was Bobby Dix. I grew up with his nephews Lee and Wade Dix in Prahran in Melbourne, and I knew Bobby and his brother Billy.

Bobby drank in various pubs in Prahran. In 1972 me, Terry 'The Tank', 'Cowboy Johnny' Harris and Dave the Jew were punching on with another group of young chaps in the Prahran commission flats when Bobby Dix staggered up and tried to break up the fight. We told him to piss off, and in a loud voice he announced he was going to call the police. And sure enough, he rushed off to the phone box. Me and the rest of my crew followed, not believing he meant to do it. But he was serious. We dragged him out of the phone box and told him we'd kick his arse if he tried to do it.

He might have had a big reputation on the waterfront, but I always remembered Bobby's attempt to call the cops on a bunch of kids. I spit on the old dog's grave.

On the day Pat Shannon got blown away, Machine Gun Bobby was supposed to be acting as his bodyguard. When Billy Longley sat in the dock on trial for the murder of Pat Shannon, 'Putty Nose' Nicholls lunged at the dock and spat at Billy, screaming, 'I hope you get life, Longley.'

So much for the rock solid, moral character of the Victorian Federated Ship Painters and Dockers.

Peter Vaitos

PETER Vaitos, known as the 'Silver Gun Rapist' was a man who terrorised the women of Melbourne in the 1970s. A burglar who raped women at gunpoint.

In November 1980 he was sentenced to 28 years with a minimum of 25 after he was convicted on 10 counts of rape, one of buggery, three of aggravated burglary, one of assault occasioning bodily harm, one of attempted rape and one of burglary.

IT'S no secret I've never had much time for sex offenders of any sort, and child molesters have never enjoyed the best of health if they have the misfortune to be put near me in jail. But one sex offender I did know and didn't mind as a bloke was Peter Vaitos, the 'Silver Gun Rapist'.

Vaitos used to cut my hair in Pentridge for a while. We used to get talking, and one day he told me a story about one of his rapes. It concerned a very posh woman in her 30s who was rather beautiful. The way he told it she returned from playing tennis one day to find him robbing her house. She was outraged, and flew into a fit of verbal abuse, as it seems she had been the victim of three previous burglaries.

Vaitos then raped her. He said she surrendered to the attack and didn't struggle — which is hardly surprising, as he had her at gunpoint. Then, as he was leaving with the various valuables he had picked out she said, 'Can you leave the television — it's a Blaupunkt.' So Peter left it, and it turned out later that he was never charged with that offence, because the woman never reported it.

Of course, that's the way he told the story. In spite of his various yarns regarding his rapes and burglaries one was left in some doubt as to their truth, because he made rape sound funny. And I know there is nothing funny about rape. But then again, I make violence sound funny, and apart from the black comedy, in reality there was little to laugh about from the other fellow's point of view. It's hard to smile with no teeth.

However, in relation to Peter Vaitos, he did seem to have a way with the female prison staff. I couldn't see the attraction myself, as Peter is a rather ugly bastard at the best of times. But he did have a winning way with females.

I often saw female prison officers making a fuss of Vaitos. One seemed very friendly, indeed. She later left the prison service.

Another thing about Vaitos was that he also had the strongest, most powerful hands of any man I'd ever met. If he grabbed hold of your wrists — and he was quite skilful at catching a wrist in each hand — you were powerless to break free of his grip. He did this once to me in jest, and I said, 'You've got rapist's hands, Peter. How could any female break free if I can't?' He was a strange fellow. And for some odd reason I cannot explain I didn't mind the bloke. But don't hold that against me.

Vaitos told me that I had once shot up a party he was at in Prahran in 1973, and just missed him with a bullet. I don't remember the event, but Peter swears it was me. I forget. I can't remember every 'shoot 'em up'.

Liking Peter Vaitos does not mean that I agreed with what he did. Much to my outrage I was once charged with rape myself. I was acquitted, but Mad Charlie was convicted. I was simply in the house with Charlie at the time. The girl he supposedly 'raped' was a prostitute and it didn't look like rape to me, as I do not agree with rape.

Drago Komljenovic

DRAGO Komljenovic has been considered a major dealer in drugs. In 1992 he was convicted of heroin trafficking. He is better known in the underworld as 'American Dave'. Police allege that Komljenovic was the ringleader of a syndicate which dealt in heroin for ten years. The gang used an electronic pager system as part of the distribution network around Melbourne.

A MAN they call 'American Dave' has been a key player in the Melbourne crime and drug world for many years. His reputation is based more on rumour than fact. He is a high flyer who lived well and certainly gave the impression of great wealth.

He was a hero to half the junkie prostitutes in Melbourne for a long while. As a heavy, his name did not really apply, but his name was well known.

No self-respecting crook was frightened of him. But in the teenage crime scene, with the parlour girls and the street whores, his name was mentioned only in whispered tones. He was considered to be more a high-profile street dealer than a top level drug boss.

But whatever the real truth about American Dave, he certainly has built a reputation.

When the son of the Australian country singer, Noel Watson, died of a drug overdose on May 3, 1990, it was rumoured to be on the orders of American Dave. It was also rumoured that the victim of the overdose, James Watson, owed American Dave more money than he could afford to pay.

Margaret was a friend of the Watson family and had driven James home on the day of his death. She was called to the inquest.

Drugs and the death they bring can touch us all. Big, small, rich and poor.

Peter Walker

PETER John Walker was the man who escaped with Ronald Ryan in December 1965. During the escape a prison officer was shot dead. Ryan was hanged for the officer's murder. Walker was sentenced to 12 years after being found guilty of manslaughter. He was sentenced to a further 12 years for the manslaughter of tow truck driver Arthur James Henderson, who was killed in an Albert Park public toilet on Christmas Eve 1965. Walker was released from prison in 1984 after serving nearly 20 years' jail. Harold Peckman was convicted of the tomahawk murders of Albert Taylor and his pregnant wife, Kathleen, in 1970. He was released in 1992.

PETER Walker, of Ryan and Walker fame, was in B Division with me in 1975. He spent a lot of time with Harold Peckman, the axe murderer. Peckman's criminal career before the axe murder conviction consisted of the theft and sale of lawn mowers — and that is not a comical remark. The man used to pinch people's lawn mowers.

In jail Peckman used to swagger about on the strength of his big axe-murderer reputation. However, as soon as violence broke out in B Division, Harold used to scurry off to his cell, never to be seen, with Peter Walker close on his heels. Walker lived in prison on nothing but the reputation and 'past glory' he got from the escape and with Ryan and Ryan's hanging. The only reason Ryan took Walker with him was that Walker had convinced him that he was a top driver and car thief — a claim which Ryan later found to be not quite true.

An interesting thing about Walker is that he spent a lot of time in the Governor's office having chit chats. He and Harold Peckman became involved with Craig 'Slim' Minogue — and then were quite chatty to police about the Russell Street bombing.

Nifty Nat

'NIFTY Nat' is another old Melbourne gangster who built himself a reputation on bluff and bullshit. He was one of the crew that hung on the coat-tails of Brian and Les Kane. When the Kanes passed wind those boys breathed deeply.

Personally, I always considered Nat to be a two-bob comedy criminal who watched too much television. Rumour has it that he was once paid $5,000 to kill me and blew the money at the races. Ha ha.

Nat often took the credit for the murder or disappearance of various criminal figures, hinting that he was in the know or somehow involved. I discovered this when I once overheard him take full credit for a missing gentleman I had personally put away. Since the death of the Kanes, Nat has kept a lower than low profile. Without the Kanes he could hardly rely on his own guts and gunfire to survive. I saw Nat and other hangers-on who hid behind the Kanes as a team of mice standing in the shadow of two rats. 'No-events', all of them.

Nobody Nick

'NOBODY Nick' is another name in the Melbourne crime scene for no other reason than he comes from a criminal family. He is what I would call a 'mouth' and a 'pack runner'. He took Keithy Faure's side against me during the Overcoat War in Pentridge, but only verbally. He is now involved in drugs — meaning up his arm — which makes him nothing to worry about. Not that he ever was.

I think Nobody's only claim to fame was that he once beat a fairly tough crook in a fight in B Division years ago — but the crook was a shooter, not a fighter. However, in spite of the fact that Nobody is a criminal nonevent — a glorified purse snatcher — he somehow built himself a rather large reputation in the underworld, and I'm buggered if I know how he did it.

I kicked Nobody up the bum in H Division and he ran screaming to tell people later on that he punched on with me for over an hour. The only friends he has are whoever has a spoon and a needle. Drugs have done one good thing. They have separated the men from the boys.

I cannot in all honesty remember a single thing Nobody Nick ever did worth mentioning.

Francis Ballis

FRANCIS Heatherington Ballis was another well-known Melbourne crook, a member of the Painters and Dockers and a good friend of Ray Chuck's. Franny had a violent and feared reputation as a gunman on the waterfront. He wrote himself into local criminal history as the man who pinched the Painters and Dockers ballot box during the elections when Billy 'The Texan' Longley was running against Pat Shannon. I think it was early 1973. Jimmy Barley was meant to be guarding the ballot box, but bullets flew and little Franny pinched it.

The box was recovered, but the strange thing was that it had been stuffed with Shannon votes. Les Kane later said to Billy Longley, 'Not that it matters now, Bill, but you won the election.' The Texan told me later that even though he was most annoyed at the time he was forced to see the funny side of little Franny running down the street with the bloody ballot box.

I got on well with old Tommy Ballis, Franny's father. He worked as a barman at the Royal Oak hotel in Richmond and he knew blokes who sold me a few guns. Old Tommy is dead now, but he was a good style of a bloke.

The last time I saw Franny he was lying unconscious in the doorway of the Station Hotel in Greville Street, Prahran after being knocked out by Cowboy Johnny Harris in 1973. People were stepping over him to get in and out of the pub. Little Franny could fight, but if the Cowboy got in the first punch it was lights out every time. Poor Johnny Harris didn't even know who he had knocked out. It was quite a funny sight. However, I will say that Franny Ballis was one chap who had guts and dash and personal courage. Why he backed up Shannon and his crew of nitwits is beyond me. Even Ray Chuck said that taking Shannon's side proved to be a mistake.

Stanley Taylor

STANLEY Taylor was an armed robber before armed robbery became fashionable. In the 1960s he robbed seven banks in five days. He escaped from jail twice and was a leader in a series of riots in H Division.

Ronald Ryan, the last man hanged in Australia, had asked Taylor to escape with him. Taylor refused and Peter Walker went over the wall in his place.

Taylor was released from prison in 1978 after serving 17 years jail. He became a youth welfare worker and part-time actor, appearing in Cop Shop *and* Prisoner.

On March 27, 1986, a stolen car packed with gelignite exploded outside the Russell Street police station. A young policewoman, Angela Taylor,

*received horrendous injuries in the explosion. She died from her wounds.
Stan Taylor, the man who said he had reformed and wanted to keep young
people away from crime, was arrested as the ringleader of the bombing. He
was the brains behind the gang, which had been responsible for a spate of
crimes, including armed robberies, leading up to the bombing.*

*Taylor broke the underworld's rules and tried to cut a deal with the
police.*

THERE are a lot of crime figures who rose and fell overnight and yet
their reputations linger like the stink that hangs on in a railway station
toilet. One of these 'big-name' non-events is Stan Taylor, now doing a
life sentence in Pentridge over the Russell Street bombing.

I always liked Billy Taylor, Stan's brother. He had guts and dash.
However, 'big, bad Stan' was a conman and a bluff merchant with a
natural skill at making younger criminals trust in him and hold him in
respect. He conned younger men into fighting his fights and doing
what he didn't have the guts to do, and when the shit hit the fan Stan
would always turn dog and give them up. That is the game he played
and the tactic he used. After the Russell Street bombing his only
problem was he was too late ... his righthand man and old friend Paul
Hetzel had got in first and done a deal by giving everyone up.

'Stan the Man' tried to battle on, thinking that pointing the finger at
one and all would save him. But he outsmarted himself. Taylor was the
heavy thinker behind the whole mess, but he got beaten to the punch.
He planned to betray the whole crew and now he is doing the lot in
Pentridge. There are never ever any prizes for turning dog second. It is
first past the post in the lag stake, with no place dividend, and Hetzel
got there first. Stan shouldn't complain because that's the game he loved
to play. Treachery.

CHAPTER 25

REMATCH: THE COURTROOM DIARIES

'HEINRICH HIMMLER'S BROTHER-IN-LAW HAS
BEEN APPOINTED JURY FOREMAN. I THINK I
AM IN DEEP SHIT.'

AFTER Read's first trial over allegedly shooting Sid Collins finished in a stalemate, both sides went off to prepare for the rematch. Read was one who would never give up a legal fight, no matter what the odds. In fact, he loved the cut and thrust of a legal joust. After all, he was the man who had shot and killed Melbourne drug dealer, Siam Ozerkam, outside a disco — in front of several witnesses who were prepared to swear that it was cold-blooded murder — yet was acquitted. Read walked on the basis of a legal argument that he swore he killed 'Sammy The Turk' in self defence. As he said later, 'God Bless Juries. I would always rather be judged by 12 than carried by six.' It did not seem to worry Read that over a two-week period in October 1992, his whole future would be decided by the 12 people who would make up the jury in the Supreme Court of Tasmania. It was time for him to fight for his life ... legally.

WE are now ready for the second trial. The Director of Public Prosecutions, Mr Damian Bugg, atop his white horse, with the sword of justice in his hand, is ready to mount the steps of the Supreme Court to slay the mainland monster.

To me this is a matter of the highest trivia, but Mr Bugg knows he must protect the good people of Tasmania. He is ready to do battle with the forces of evil.

On my side is the lovely Anita Betts, my lawyer. I am sure we can all look forward to about two weeks of legal fun and hilarity.

The Crown case, if you can call it that, seems to be based on a story hastily put together by two men I once trusted, Trent Anthony and Sid Collins. According to them I hunted Sid down for four days to murder him on the orders of the Hell's Angels in Melbourne.

I then wounded Collins and rushed him to hospital in a mercy dash, then raced home to bury the weapon in my own backyard.

If Collins and Anthony are to be believed, I am the only gunman in Australia who provides an after sales service in the form of a medical plan. What rot.

THEY have just sworn in the jury, eight woman and four men. I nearly had an all-female jury, but the Crown challenged so we ended up with four rather dull-looking gentlemen.

I thought I was in luck when one chick, a big girl covered in jewellery from neck to ankle and dressed to thrill, walked in with her girlfriend. Both of them got the chatters and the giggles as they looked in my direction, but the Crown challenged them.

So now I have eight ladies ranging from a glamorous blonde, a big-eyed gentle-looking lady, a couple of young girls, one who looks quite smart and the other seeming to be wondering why she is here, a woman who looks like she is from the Save the Gay Whales Movement, a couple of housewives and a pig ugly cow, who looks like she wants to fight me. The blokes are a collection of oddbods. One looks like Heinrich Himmler's brother-in-law. Ha ha.

So, all in all, your pretty typical jury. I have my false teeth in my pocket in case I am called upon to smile broadly. I believe in the jury system and trust I will get a fair go. I would rather be judged by 12 than carried by six any day.

Anita is adopting her convent schoolgirl approach, as a female jury can be a bit harsh on lady lawyers. Meanwhile, I sit in the dock with Edith Piaf's famous song 'No Regrets' dancing in my head. I am ready to do battle.

I KNOW it must be terribly boring for people to hear Chopper Read say, 'Hey, I didn't do this one.' I know it would be more fun for me to say, 'Yeah, yeah, I shot another one,' and then go into the blood and guts details of how I did it.

However, even if I am convicted of this shooting, I won't be able to say I really did it.

I wish I had done it, because then we wouldn't be going through this courtroom drama as Collins would simply be on the missing list. The point is that I did not shoot Collins in the back of my car and I did not drive him to hospital.

I didn't shoot Sid Collins, or anyone else for that matter, with a 9mm Beretta, and I have my doubts that he was even shot with a Beretta.

I know that Chopper Read saying he didn't shoot someone is a first. However, regardless of the fact that everyone seems to take my guilt for granted, I must deny involvement in this whole fiasco. I don't know what more I can say about this matter.

As this case unfolds, some of the people who are convinced of my guilt may begin to suspect some funny business. They may as well hang me on the wall and call me Mona Lisa, as they already have me framed.

I sincerely believe I can win this and expose the truth, but I know that with my record and my luck, I could be found guilty.

It is a novel experience for me to actually tell people I didn't shoot someone.

Day one

THE game has begun.

One of the housewives on the jury has bailed out so they got some old rough nut in as a replacement. That makes it five men and seven women.

Sid 'never tell a lie' Collins is spewing out his evidence. I suspect that he has been to some Crown witness charm school as he has improved from the first trial. He is all smiles and appears to be relaxed and polished. I almost believe him myself. However, the polish may tarnish when Anita, the human vampire, bites him on the neck. She drew blood last time. But, watching her now, she looks really pissed off.

The funny thing is that although my neck is on the chopping block, I must admit I love every second of it. I really enjoy a good courtroom battle. I'm a war monger and I love a good shit fight and so does Anita Betts. I can hear her teeth grinding with rage as she sits there with her legs crossed, waiting to attack.

This is no longer a simple court case. I love it all.

Day two

TODAY Sid 'Trust Me' Collins was still in fine form until Madam Lash ripped into him in no uncertain terms and did indeed tarnish the polish. He told the court he had consulted a lawyer re the possibility of suing me through the civil courts. I suspect he has dreams of putting his hands on Captain Chopper's treasure. Yo, Ho, Ho and a bottle of rum. The poor deluded fool.

Then came Trent 'I'm on Sid's side' Anthony, who told the court that the reason his memory had improved was that he had been reading up on his notes since the last trial.

I don't know if young Trent is a nightmare or a blessing. The kid is not known for deep thought. He continues his evidence tomorrow.

As for Collins, he denied to the court that he had ever asked me to kill the Groper, and said he had been on the phone to him only a week ago. The plot thickens.

PS: Heinrich Himmler's brother-in-law has been appointed jury foreman. I think I am in deep shit. Ha, ha.

Day three

DAY three finished yesterday and I have the weekend to reflect on the future. I am lying back enjoying the thin Tassie sun in the remand yard.

Kelli, Mad Micky Marlow's girlfriend, came to visit. She said the two of them were thinking of me last night as they frolicked in the spa bath, guzzling champagne and playing funny buggers with the baby oil.

I hope they drop the electric hair dryer in the bloody spa. I hate these 'having a good time, wish you were here' remarks when you're in the middle of a life-and-death court battle. I sometimes lose my sense of humour.

Anita had a go at Trent Anthony yesterday and I thought turned him into a gibbering mess of confusion. He was last seen fleeing the court steps with his police minders. I have no idea why they keep him under such strict control. One feels they think he may run into a Jewish problem.

We whizzed through six more Crown Witnesses. The police witnesses, forensic and ballistic evidence begins on Monday. Anita and her all-female staff are all firing up in the defence. Chopper's Angels, God bless them.

There is a sweet old lady who sits in the back of the court every day. She was there all through the last trial. Some people mistake her for my mother as she is always smiling at me, bless her heart.

The police have returned all my guns to my father, just before the re-trial. That's Tassie: mad one day, totally insane the next.

I was asked to autograph three books during an adjournment. I don't know whether I should laugh or cry. If you told a donkey this, it would kick you in the head for telling tall stories.

Day four

I LOVE the smell of a courtroom in the morning. Ha ha. It is Monday morning and it is day four of the trial and I am off to court. I am almost physically ill with worry.

I rang Margaret and she feels the same. For her, it is the worry of losing me. For me, it is the worry of being beaten by these mice. The thought of that is so humiliating.

We are scoring more points than we did in the last trial, but I am still concerned.

As I was getting ready to leave, the remand yard comedian yelled out, 'Chopper, Stop!' I looked around and he was putting on a mad drag act, a fairly good impression of Diana Ross singing 'Stop In The Name Of Love'. Falsetto voice and swinging hips, the lot.

He looks like a cross between an unmade bed and five miles of bad road. I am embarrassed to say that he also comes from Melbourne. It was, however, a very funny sight.

The other day he told me that Adolf Hitler had a fake arm he kept so that he could give the fascist salute at big rallies without getting tired. I was amazed until everyone began to laugh, the bastard.

But now it is back to the worry of the court. This case is changing me. I am starting to feel the emotion of anger.

The people doing this to me are not forward thinkers.

MARGARET puts Mr Nibbles, the world famous staffy-pit bull cross, on the phone to me and he barks. With no children I suppose Mr Nibbles is the next best thing.

Margaret told me that Billy The Texan has been taking her out. They go ballroom dancing. She sits and watches and old Billy trips the light fantastic. That would be a sight I would love to see.

Day four of the trial is over and the only friendly faces in the courtroom are those of the little old lady at the back and my old mate, Big Bill Watson, who has been in every day.

Anita remains confident but I sense impending doom. The jury has taken on a high moral tone and are starting to look and dress like invitation-only guests at the Bishop's tea party.

I just don't know what to make of them.

Damian Bugg is a man possessed. He reminds me of God's avenging angel. With his lofty position and the players on his team that he has to call on, he has the courtroom appearance of a master craftsman.

I don't know what Mr Justice Cox is making of all this. I hope he is not as confused as I am. Anita only gets better under pressure and the pressure is on now in a big way

Day five tomorrow. The Crown has cut back its witness list, some of the duds from the last trial have been fired.

The game continues.

Day five

BY the end of the day I am nearly punch drunk from listening to the never-ending evidence from the Crown. One copper did agree that I was one of the old-fashioned criminals who didn't give people up in police stations and that I had denied the offence. This seemed to contradict some other evidence that had been given earlier.

Trent Anthony claimed that while drinking at the Clarendon Arms Hotel with me and Collins he had placed a bet through Mick Alexander's telephone account on a certain horse at a certain time. He said it won and he had been paid out. But a TAB lady called by the Crown on some other matters brought records showing that the horse had not won. It was only a small point for us, but he used it as a time gauge, so that was a point for us. I just hope the jury wasn't as punch drunk as I feel, and that they noticed the point.

This trial is like a mental sledge hammer.

Interesting to note that the police have said that they found the gun in my backyard while I was in custody as a result of information received. Trent Anthony has admitted that he told the police where to find the gun.

I suspect the trial is beginning to take its toll on little Anita. But she keeps telling me to cheer up and not to lose my temper.

Day six

DAY six of the trial is over. The sweet old dear who sits in the back of the court every day is named Beryl, and she is a lovely old girl. Anita was cross at me for not having a shave, so I have to be all cleaned up tomorrow for when I give evidence.

Anita and Damian Bugg seem to be talking to each other in a civil manner. In fact, old Buggsy is acting like a thorough gent. I don't like it at all. I prefer evil looks and cold hate rather than fake politeness and forced civility. I said to Anita today, 'What is he trying to do, sink us or sell us a used car?'

The DNA expert took the stand again today. DNA should be kept to the Family Courts to decided which kid belongs to which dad and so on. But in the criminal courts, it is a waste of time.

'The blood stain marked Exhibit A could belong to Mr X or five to 15 per cent of the population.' Every nitwit scientific idea that ever came out of America, Australia grabs on to like it is the miracle cure.

DNA is high-class voodoo, witch doctor stuff. I have been losing hope, but Anita tells me we could get up on this, wait and see. Anita and the people who work with her are far from fools, believe me.

There is a fine scientific point that I have brought to Anita's attention, involving the angle of the bullet entry and exit points in the car. I have been allowed to check the car personally. I suspect I have them on a good scientific point, but science is a contradiction. Trying to get a Crown scientific or ballistic expert to answer a straight question is like trying to pull chicken's teeth.

Day seven

DAY seven of the trial is over. I had the judge, the prosecutor, the ballistic expert for the Crown and Anita all down in the Supreme Court garage crawling in and out of the car, pulling out the back seat, poking probes in here and out there to test angles of entry.

I was trying to prove that the angle of entry and exit in the back seat of the car proved that he could not have been shot by anyone sitting in the front left-hand side. The prosecution objected and the judge didn't allow it. At any rate the back seat was ripped out of the car, thus making the test pointless. I gave up the idea. I hope the jury got the point.

I am now giving my evidence. I told the jury that had I shot Sid Collins, I would have shot him in the driveway, as he came home late. I would have used the same method as was used to kill the Australian Federal Police Assistant Commissioner, Colin Winchester, in the driveway of his house. I told the jury it was an old trick but a goody.

I told the jury that my preferred weapon was a sawn-off .410

shotgun. Trent carried one under the front seat of the car. The jury seemed to be lapping it up. I talk straight and I talk sense. Win, lose or draw I will give them something to think about.

I suspect that the police, the Crown, the Judge, and definitely the jury, have never seen anything like me before. Ha, ha.

A court battle is a massive game of chess, and Damian Bugg is no Bobby Fischer. As for Trent Anthony and Sid Collins, they couldn't beat me in a game of snakes and ladders.

I am not beaten yet.

Day eight

IT'S Friday, and Buggsy had me in the witness box all day. At the luncheon adjournment I gave him a shifty wink and a smile and he replied with a nod and a sly grin. After the adjournment we again exchanged nods and sly smiles, like two battleworn veterans who had fought each other to a near standstill.

My anger, hate and rage had turned into a sort of sneaking regard. The summing up begins on Monday and I no longer hold ill-will towards Mr Damian Bugg. Win, lose or draw he went for the kill and didn't weaken. Guts, brains and dash — he went in on me boots and all, and I respect that.

I've been playing poker with him and all his Crown witnesses. They have all held a fist full of aces, and I have held no cards at all. But I've given Damian Bugg a courtroom battle he won't soon forget.

I am prepared for a guilty verdict. It's the fight that counts more than the verdict. It has been a bloody great fight. When that one great scorer comes to mark against our time it is not if we won or lost but how we played the game. If I win this, it won't be Buggsy's fault. If I lose, it won't be Anita's fault. Buggsy spent half the day using my own book against me. That's what General George Paton did before he went against Rommel, 'the Desert Fox'. He read Rommel's book. The cunning swine.

I HAVE always been a bit superstitious. I believe in good luck and bad luck. Sid Collins was shot on the 13th of the fifth month, and the jury looks like being asked to go out and consider their verdict on the 13th. I don't like that. Also, one of the young girls on my jury looks like, and reminds me of, Miss Lina Galea. Young Lina went missing in 1987. I didn't kill her. Nor did I bury her mortal remains, despite some unkind rumours. But Ricky Parr and Lina Galea, a Maltese drug addict, went on the missing list because they were a part of Phillip 'The Iceman' Wilson's neo-Nazi fun club.

I didn't know Lina, but I briefly met her once in January 1987. She was a sad cross between a hippy, peace-freak, love child and a drug-crazed junkie. When I met Lina she was crying and in trouble. She had this sad look in her eyes. This chick on the jury has the same face and eyes as young Lina. It is very spooky. It is as if the ghost of Lina is sitting on my jury. It is bad luck.

Why should Lina's ghost be dirty on me. I didn't kill her. Then again, I could have helped her. But I could have, and I didn't. I don't like to sit in court, look at the jury and see the face of a dead person.

I AM told that Sid 'Never Tell A Lie' Collins has packed up his bags and baggage and taken his new wife Simone, young son, dogs and cats and cocky in a cage and fled to parts unknown. I am reliably informed that he is no longer in Tasmania, but has left his friends who stood by him in this outrage against my good self to remain behind and either live in hiding or fight the good fight should I win my court case.

Cowards die a thousand deaths but there will be no fight. I don't have to lift a finger. Their own paranoia will cripple them. As for Mr

Collins, he will spend the rest of his days wondering, waiting and watching forever on guard in a nightmare world of paranoid suspicion, panic, tension and stress. In his dreams at night he will hear my voice behind him in the dark. 'Hello Sid, how's your kidney?' Ha ha.

I did not shoot Sid Collins but he does know that if I ever see him again that I could take a turn for the worse and demand that he donate his remaining kidney to medical science. May he run far and hide well, living his life in paranoid hell.

I may be found guilty, but at least I can look myself in the mirror while Sid Collins will live his life waiting for the axe to fall. I am one man alone. I have no army to call upon. The only soldiers I have are the phantoms I command to dance in the paranoid minds of my enemies.

News of Trent Anthony is rather ordinary. Still in the Launceston area, with police minders on tap if needed, his idea of hiding is a pair of dark glasses and a long raincoat. Ha ha. It's all their own doing.

Day nine

WITH day nine of the trial over Buggsy and me exchanged polite nods of the head again. Then he launched into a closing address that would have hung ten men. Last time around he gave it a lick and a promise; this time he left no stone unturned. I suspect that, but for the grace of God, Damian Bugg would have made a bloody good toecutter. The man has a cold-blooded attitude that I admire.

As for Anita. What can I say? She put her heart and soul into a closing address full of emotion. No lawyer has ever fought a case as hard as this woman, and come what may I owe her a great deal. She is a great lady and with only five or so years as a lawyer under her belt, she is on her way up, believe me.

His Honour, Mr Justice Cox, is summing up. He will be done by tomorrow, the 13th, when the jury will be sent out. He calls me 'Read' and I doubt he's running for president of the Chopper Read fan club. God help me. Anita's closing address was heavy on logic and common sense. A woman can grasp logic and common sense quicker than a man.

Damian Bugg's closing address was more a case of 'Look, members of the jury. There's Chopper Read. Quick, lock him up.' Crude but effective.

Several members of the jury appear to be falling asleep. Or they're on medication. Ha ha.

Day ten

TODAY is October 13. One way or the other I reckon I will receive the jury's answer today. The Lina Galea lookalike stares at me, and the 13th has always been the devil's day for me. I doubt that Bobby Fischer could get himself out of this chess game. This is the most important legal battle of my life, as it will in many ways decide my life. If I go under it will draw the curtain on my relationship with Margaret. I will always love her, and I will keep in touch. But I will have to let her go to live her own life. Loving me has only brought her torment and pain.

I can tell you that I didn't shoot Sid Collins. Yes, I suspected he was going to get shot. Yes, I even feel I know who pulled the trigger. I even know why. But I did not know that my own gun was to be used, or that it would magically appear in my backyard, or that Trent Anthony and Sid Collins would twist the plot and do an Alfred Hitchcock on me. Ah well, as old Ned said, such is life.

For all the ones I got away with, am I now to go under on the only one I didn't do? I will soon know.

I have found that master legal craftsman Damian Bugg has a stern young female offsider who has yet to understand the subtleties of legal jousting. She gives me icy looks of disapproval like a Sunday school teacher in fancy dress. Cute, if you like that sort of thing.

Anyway, if I do get a jail sentence out of this, I'll try to get a job in the prison kitchen. I'll whizz them up a curry that will burn their bums so bad they will feel like 'blue-eyed boys' in a Turkish prison.

I ESCAPED the 13th without harm, so it's back again tomorrow. When the jury went out to consider the verdict at 1.20 pm today (and they have been sent to one of Hobart's better hotels for the night) they were still arguing the toss. Being locked away for the night is not a common happening down here. Juries are generally back with a verdict in two to six hours. Some onlooker asked Anita today why I didn't get one of the local, heavyweight lawyers — a rather insulting remark, I felt. In my experience all or most of the top legal talent and all or most of the talent in the Department of Public Prosecutions are all part of the local old boys' network ... same private schools, same golf clubs, same charities or committees. In Tassie, like everywhere else, it's a case of the Good Old Boy Network. Hiring Anita was a tactical move on my part because of a healthy distrust of the old school tie network. We have fought the case pure and simple with a pocket full of nothing. My only defence is that I didn't do it. I don't know what to think any more.

The screws at the court tell me that the girls in the Supreme Court typing pool believe that I didn't do it, bless their little hearts. Come what may, Anita and me have given these buggers a hell of a fight.

One pleasant thing is that while waiting in the court cells I have a lovely fisherman's basket with all the trimmings and extras for my evening meal. Very nice indeed. Much better than curry in H Division.

Day 11

THE jury went back to the hotel again tonight ready for the 12th day tomorrow. I think they are all playing lounge chair detective — deer stalker hats, the lot. The men think they are Sherlock Holmes, the ladies are in their Agatha Christie mode.

I can't believe it: my only defence is that I didn't do it. I wasn't there, and I'm being set up. So the honesty of Collins and Anthony must be in question. Anita and her legal secretary Narelle spent several hours with me downstairs in the cells — I should say in the legal interview room — just to keep me company. We talked cops and robbers, legal tactics and strategy and general courtroom comedy. I enjoyed myself.

I no longer know what to think. I feel that yes, maybe I could win. But then I say to myself: why should I be so lucky? I pace the cell haunted with the thought of this case and the thought of the jury returning with a guilty verdict. Well, I will see what tomorrow brings.

My one ray of sunshine is the thought of Buggsy pacing his office as I pace the court cell. Ha ha.

Day 12

IT'S over. The foreman of the just stood up and said 'Guilty'. I felt more sorry for Anita than I did for myself. I've never seen any lawyer put up a tougher, harder fight than that wonderful lady.

As for me, finding me guilty is all very well. Sentencing me to jail naturally follows. However, in the state of Tasmania they don't have a jail — they've only got Risdon — so a miscarriage of justice is followed by a total comedy. Shaken, but not stirred. Ha ha. I'll tell you this for nothing. With only one kidney left and a drinking problem, Sid Collins won't outlive me, that's for sure. Ha ha.

Damian Bugg jumped to his feet and asked the judge to consider giving me an indeterminate sentence under the Dangerous Offenders Act. Call it what you will, 'Governor's Pleasure' or 'the key'. While my eyes remain dry, my heart cries for little Margaret. She's heartbroken. Well, it does seem the ghosts of my criminal past — crimes unsolved and crimes unpunished have gathered together to get me for the one that I didn't do. Bloody marvellous.

The cute little Lina Galea lookalike had a sad look in her eye as I stood in the dock. She was one of the 'not guilty, I'm sure' brigade. When I got back to my cell at Risdon, I had a letter waiting for me from Renee Brack wishing me all the best. She's a nice lady.

I have had a pair of lucky socks I wore at the last trial. I burnt them on the heater in my cell and had to toss them out before the second trial. Fantastic.

GOD doesn't like drug dealers. He might forgive a junkie, but he won't forgive a drug dealer. I could kill a thousand of the human mice and still walk through heaven's door. A lot of people who believe in God have grown very la-de-da. I'm more of an Old Testament man myself with a leaning to fire and brimstone. What's a blowtorch on the feet compared with the fires of hell. Damian Bugg expected me to hang my head in shame, because I've killed a few scumbags.

Did I do the wrong thing? Not likely. My only shame is that I didn't get to kill more of the arsewipes. The killing and torture of these vermin should not only be made legal, it should be made compulsory. Murder should be a five-bob fine when it comes to the topic of drug dealers. Forget the dealers and the assorted mice for a minute and think of the children of the nation. They are killing themselves in the gutters of the cities, or selling their bums in the backlanes and streets of our suburbs, all to make the rats of the drug world rich and powerful men.

Ashamed? Of course I am. Because I'm inside and there's many of them still out there. I should have killed more of the scum when I was in the underworld. For that, and only that, I beg humble forgiveness.

Damian Bugg, and prosecutors in general, see themselves as

protecting society from people like me. But, in the end, who are they really protecting?

THE END

So now you've read my second book,
I wonder what you think?
Did you get through all the pages,
Without the aid of a drink?
I know a lot of you must hate me,
With a venom and a rage,
Damning me to hell,
As you turn each bloody page,
I know I'm a bit rough,
I'm neither smooth nor groovy,
And if you didn't like the book,
You'll hate the bloody movie.
Ha, ha ha.

THE EDITORS

In early 1991, investigative journalist John Silvester interviewed Mark Brandon Read in Pentridge Prison's top security H Division for a series of reports in the *Herald-Sun*. Over the next two years, Read wrote almost daily to Silvester from both inside and outside jails. These letters formed the basis of Read's best-selling autobiography, *Chopper*, and this sequel, *How to Shoot Friends and Influence People*.

Silvester has been a Melbourne-based crime reporter since 1978. In 1990, he worked for the *Sunday Times* Insight team in London. He is co-author of *Inside Victoria: A Chronicle of Scandal* with Bob Bottom.

Andrew Rule is a former chief police reporter for *The Age*, feature writer for *The Herald* and television documentary producer. He is currently the producer of Melbourne radio 3AW's breakfast programme. His previous works include *Cuckoo*, the factual account of the 'Mr Stinky' murder investigation. He co-edited Read's first book.

The editors would like to thank criminologist Rick T. Bloke and psychologist J. H. C. Smith for their guidance.